CITYSPOTS
NICE

Paul Medbourne

Written by Paul Medbourne
Updated by Kathryn Tomasetti

Published by Thomas Cook Publishing
A division of Thomas Cook Tour Operations Limited
Company registration No: 1450464 England
The Thomas Cook Business Park, 9 Coningsby Road
Peterborough PE3 8SB, United Kingdom
Email: books@thomascook.com, Tel: +44 (0)1733 416477
www.thomascookpublishing.com

Produced by The Content Works Ltd
Aston Court, Kingsmead Business Park, Frederick Place
High Wycombe, Bucks HP11 1LA
www.thecontentworks.com

Series design based on an original concept by Studio 183 Limited

ISBN: 978-1-84157-873-6

First edition © 2006 Thomas Cook Publishing
This second edition © 2008 Thomas Cook Publishing
Text © Thomas Cook Publishing
Maps © Thomas Cook Publishing/PCGraphics (UK) Limited
Transport map © Communicarta Limited

Series Editor: Kelly Anne Pipes
Project Editor: Linda Bass
Production/DTP: Steven Collins

Printed and bound in Spain by GraphyCems

Cover photography (Apartment balconies) © Jerry Driendl/Getty Images

CONTENTS

SYMBOLS KEY

The following symbols are used throughout this book:

ⓐ address ⓣ telephone ⓕ fax ⓦ website address ⓔ email
ⓛ opening times ⓝ public transport connections

The following symbols are used on the maps:

𝒊 information office		▦ points of interest
✈ airport		○ city
✚ hospital		○ large town
🄪 police station		◦ small town
🚌 bus station		═ motorway
🚆 railway station		— main road
✝ cathedral		— minor road
❶ numbers denote featured		— railway
cafés & restaurants		

Hotels and restaurants are graded by approximate price as follows:
£ budget price ££ mid-range price £££ expensive

Abbreviations used in addresses:

av.	avenue
blvd	boulevard
espl.	esplanade
pl.	place (square)
prom.	promenade

⊙ *Head to the port for outstanding food and views*

INTRODUCING
Nice

Introduction

The undisputed queen and capital of the French Riviera, Nice is France's fifth largest city, with a permanent population of nearly 400,000 and over ten times that number of visitors annually. Nice-Côte d'Azur airport welcomes more international passengers than any other in France except Paris Charles de Gaulle. Nice began catering to overseas visitors before organised tourism was born and has seen it all, adapting in turn to the tastes of Victorian British aristocracy, *fin de siècle* Russian princes, Jazz Age American millionaires and today's city-breakers, backpackers and family holidaymakers. Tourism is more than Nice's life-blood, it's its *raison d'être*.

If there is a 'real' Nice, it's not immediately apparent. The ambience is not typically French, nor Italian, even though Nice was an Italian city until 1860 and still retains strong cultural ties to its Mediterranean neighbour. The general standard of food is excellent, and there are plenty of places where you can sample authentic Provençal and French *haute cuisine* at its best, but most of its eating places are geared to international tourist tastes. It enjoys a beautiful setting on the Baie des Anges, but has no sandy beaches of its own. The glamour of the *belle époque* and art deco can still be seen in its buildings, but today it has shed its air of exclusiveness. It has an eventful past and has attracted visits from many of the great names of the last 200 years, and some of its natives, such as Garibaldi, Masséna and Simone Weil, Holocaust survivor and first President of the European Parliament, have been prominent on the world stage, but Nice wears its history lightly.

The truth is that Nice is too laid-back to worry. Its most visible characteristic is a casual attitude to life – and it works hard to ensure that its guests are relaxed and entertained. It provides safe and lively streets, seemingly endless sunshine, a clutch of world-class galleries and museums, over 200 hotels, cuisine from all over the world and in every price bracket, vibrant nightlife and an excellent transport infrastructure. Whatever your age, budget or tastes, Nice wants you to enjoy yourself.

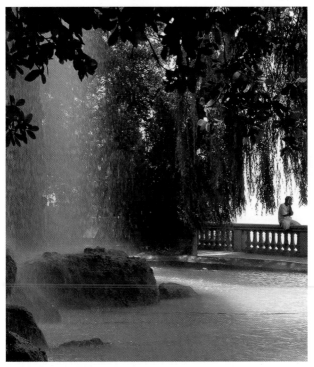

● *Relax by the waterfall of Le Château*

When to go

Nice's mild climate makes it an excellent weekend destination throughout the year. You can easily take a dip in the Med anytime between May and October, but it's best to avoid the crowds and the sky-high summer prices (of both flights and accommodation) by planning your visit during May–June or September–October.

SEASONS & CLIMATE

For the first 100 years or so of its tourism history, Nice was famed as a winter resort. Its location between the Mediterranean and the sheltering Alpes-Maritimes ensures that winter is comparatively warm (the average is 12°C/53°F December–March, and it rarely falls below 5°C/41°F) and summer not too hot (peaking in July and August at an average 24°C/75°F, though on some days it can reach around 30°C/86°F). June and September are probably the best summer months for comfortable heat.

Even in the darkest winter months expect five hours of sunshine a day, though all those mountains on the doorstep mean occasional showers: July is the best travel month for rain-haters, while October

● Nice's year-round sunshine has been a tourist magnet for 200 years

and November see the maximum rainfall, around 110 mm/4¹/₂ in.
average per month – still hardly a deluge.

ANNUAL EVENTS
February–March
Carnaval de Nice The city's premier event (see pages 12–13), held over
two weeks at Lent and culminating in a grand parade and fireworks
on the final Sunday. Ⓦ www.nicecarnaval.com
Festin des Cougourdons (Gourd Festival) A traditional festival with
local folklore and decorated gourds. Held in the Jardins de Cimiez.
Ⓦ www.cougourdon.com

April
Semi-Marathon International de Nice This half marathon is run
along the prom. des Anglais in late April. A shorter children's race
and charity race also feature. Ⓦ www.nicesemimarathon.com

May
Fête des Mai Music, picnics and folk dancing celebrate the arrival
of spring in the gardens and the Amphitheatre of Cimiez. Held on
Sundays and holidays in May.
Cannes Film Festival Head to Cannes to rub shoulders with the
glitzy and glamorous, at one of the chicest festivals on the Riviera.
Ⓦ www.festival-cannes.fr
Grand Prix de Monaco Just 25 minutes by train from Nice, a day at
Monaco's Grand Prix is a must for Formula 1 fans. Ⓦ www.formula1.com

June
Fête de la Musique Stroll through Nice's city streets on 21 June to
enjoy various bands, acoustic musicians and street performers vying

for attention during one of France's most electrifying evenings.
W www.fetedelamusique.culture.fr

Fête du Château Head up to the Colline du Château for locally
produced meats and cheeses, traditional ravioli, fruit wines and
hours of rocking music. A Niçois favourite. W www.feteduchateau.com

Fête de la Mer Fishermen celebrate St Peter's feast day, 29 June,
with a mass in the Gésu church followed by a procession to the
Ponchettes beach, where a boat is ceremonially burned.

July–August

Bastille Day 14 July is marked by fireworks on the promenade des
Anglais – grab a picnic and head down early to secure your spot
among the crowds on the beach.

Nice Jazz Festival This big open-air event is held for eight days in
July in the atmospheric surroundings of the Arènes de Cimiez
(see page 106). W www.nicejazzfest.com

Les Nuits Musicales de Nice This festival of chamber music follows on from
the Jazz Festival at the end of July and extends for two weeks in early
August (see page 106). W www.hexagone.net/music/nuits_musicales.htm

La Castellada Actors and musicians perform the history of the
Château (see page 77). ☎ 04 93 84 86 11

September

Fête du Port The streets surrounding the port are closed off to traffic
on the first Saturday in September and quickly fill with music,
drinking and dancing. Traditional wooden fishing boats give free
rides to the other side of the action.

Fête de Catherine Ségurane Defender and patron saint of Nice, local
washerwoman Catherine Ségurane caused the Turks to abandon
their 1543 siege of the city by flashing her bare bottom at them.

Join the locals in their candle-lit procession in her honour through the Old Town on 7 September.

October
Fête de Ste-Réparate Nice's Old Town celebrates its patron saint day on 7 October with masses, processions, dancing and music.

December
Régates Internationales de Star de Noël Top-level competitors contend for France's most important sailing regatta title.
🕿 04 93 89 39 78 (Club Nautique de Nice)

PUBLIC HOLIDAYS
Public transport runs to Sunday schedules, and banks, post offices and public buildings are closed on these days. Many shops (but not generally restaurants) are also closed.
Le Premier de l'an (New Year's Day) 1 Jan
Pâques (Easter) & Lundi de Pâques (Easter Monday)
23–24 Mar 2008, 12–13 Apr 2009
Fête du premier mai (Labour Day) 1 May
Fête de la Victoire (World War II Victory Day) 8 May
La Pentecôte (Pentacost/Whit Sunday) & Lundi de Pentecôte (Whit Monday) 11–12 May 2008, 31 May–1 June 2009
Fête nationale (Bastille Day) 14 July
Assomption (Assumption of the Blessed Virgin Mary) 15 Aug
La Toussaint (All Saints Day) 1 Nov
Jour d'armistice (Remembrance Day) 11 Nov
Noël (Christmas Day) 25 Dec

Carnaval in Nice

In Nice the traditional pre-Lent celebrations have turned into the Riviera's biggest tourist spectacle. The exuberant celebration of Carnaval (from Latin *carne vale*, 'goodbye to meat') was first recorded in 1294. By the 18th century the riotous street parties had given way to exclusive indoor masked balls, and Carnaval was in the doldrums. It took the imagination of local citizen Andriot Saëtone to revive the old carnival spirit and at the same time transform it into one of the greatest shows on earth. His Festival Committee organised the first modern Carnaval parade in 1873, with a presiding monarch, a straw puppet called King Carnaval I. So began the tradition of the Carnaval King, who reigns over the two weeks or more of festivities. In 1876 a Flower Parade along the seafront was added, accompanied by the elegant tossing of bouquets between the carriages of the gentry; this quickly developed into a free-for-all chucking of flower petals into the crowd. These days the people on each of the 20 floats throw an estimated 100,000 gladioli, roses, carnations and mimosas to onlookers.

Prominent cartoonists are involved in the design of the theme after which each King is named. The themes are often topical or satirical: 2007's theme was the King of Free-for-Alls, while 2008 celebrates the King of Bats, Cats, Rats and other Legendary Creatures.

The entire festival lasts over two weeks, which, although theoretically should end on Shrove Tuesday, in recent years the grand finale has taken place three to four Sundays before Easter. On the opening Saturday afternoon King Carnaval makes his entrance at the head of 20 themed floats, followed by 180 revellers wearing 'big heads' of papier mâché, accompanied by street theatre and music groups and the first Battle of the Flowers (there are several others during the festival). The programme continues with almost daily processions until the last big afternoon parade, after which, in the evening, King Carnaval marches to the beach, where his reign ends as he is ceremonially burnt.

Parades circle the promenade des Anglais, passing the seafront by the back of the opera house, and head along the quai des Etats-Unis, looping the Jardin Albert 1er and then returning through the main viewing area back along the prom. Viewing areas on the north and south sides consist of both banks of seating and standing zones. Admission to either is by ticket only, bought on the day from on-site machines or in advance either on-line at the Carnaval website, Ⓦ www.nicecarnaval.com (up to 48 hours beforehand), or at the tourist office, ⓐ 5 prom. des Anglais. Rates for 2008 vary from €30 per person for a seat at the main opening and closing parades down to €8 for the standing enclosure mid-week.

The 2008 dates are 16 February–2 March; for a full calendar of events see Ⓦ www.nicecarnaval.com.

▲ *Life's one long parade at Carnaval time*

History

Greek traders founded Nikaia, 'City of Victory', in the fourth century BC near the modern port, but the area had already been inhabited for hundreds of thousands of years, as the finds displayed at Terra Amata (see page 101) testify. When the Romans arrived in the first century BC they preferred to build their settlement, Cemenelum, on the hill that is now the middle-class suburb of Cimiez. The Greek port became the medieval town corresponding to today's Vieille Ville. Possession of the town passed to the Italian House of Savoy, and Italian Nizza only became French Nice in 1860 by the Treaty of Turin. Remnants of the Savoy era include the ruins of the old castle of the Dukes atop the Château hill and the citadel of Villefranche (see page 114).

Nice's harbour was unsuitable for large-scale commerce, and the city might have become a backwater if 18th-century British travellers hadn't discovered its greatest asset – the climate. By 1822 the expat community was large enough to fund the construction of its own seaside walk, the promenade des Anglais. With the coming of the railway the stream of visitors became a torrent and Queen Victoria's first visit in 1895 bestowed the ultimate seal of approval.

The Russian aristocracy also felt the need to escape their own winters, and by the 1880s were buying and decorating villas, gambling and spending fortunes. Following the Russian Revolution of 1917 Nice was full of suddenly impoverished noblemen. Today's most visible reminder of the Russian invasion is the splendid Orthodox Cathedral (see pages 78–81). Just as Russian money dried up, wealthy Americans discovered the Riviera, and Nice became an expatriate capital of the Jazz Age. Belle époque style was succeeded by art deco, best evidenced in the 1927 façade of the Palais de la Méditerranée (see pages 39 and 82).

Nice's civic reputation in the years after World War II was marred by an unhealthy combination of crime, municipal corruption and ultra-right-wing politics. The return of wealthy Russian visitors, following the fall of the Soviet Union (they are once again the city's top-spending tourist nationality), has brought with it suspicions of Russian Mafia involvement in local crime. Yet Nice continues to attract an ever-increasing number of visitors, and is home to the second busiest airport in France.

LOCAL HEROES

To name a *place*, an *espace*, a *Musée*, a *Lycée* and a *rue* all after one man suggests that the locals must think highly of him. André Masséna was born in Nice in 1758 and after a brief spell in the military settled down in Nice as a shopkeeper with a sideline in smuggling. He re-enlisted after the French Revolution and reached the rank of marshal at the age of 35, serving under Napoleon as one of France's outstanding commanders until 1811, when his attempt to capture Lisbon was thwarted by the British under the Duke of Wellington. He never again held a command or returned to Nice, dying in Paris in 1817. A brilliant commander, a looter on a grand scale and a notorious womaniser, Masséna was rated by his nemesis Wellington as 'the only French commander who gave me sleepless nights'. By contrast, fellow-Niçois Garibaldi is commemorated only in a *place*, a *rue* and a statue. But then, he only reunified Italy, whereas Masséna defended France – although, owing to the changing nationality of Nice, Masséna was born an Italian and Garibaldi a Frenchman!

Lifestyle

By the end of the 19th century, Nice was among the first cities in the world whose economy depended on tourism, and catering to the foreign visitor remains its number one business today. The result is a truly cosmopolitan and tolerant atmosphere.

If you look at the names in the phone book or at the façades of the buildings in the Vieille Ville, you could believe for a moment that you were in Italy. On the other hand, the official infrastructure – police, post offices, Palais de Justice, street names – is totally French, and the iconic images of French life – citizens hurrying by with an armful of fresh *baguettes*, old ladies walking poodles – are in evidence everywhere. But wherever you stroll or sit down in central Nice, the conversations you overhear are as likely to be in English (from both sides of the Atlantic), Russian or Spanish as in French.

Perhaps it's harder to spot the residents because they enjoy much the same lifestyle as the tourists, and they have the leisure to do it – 11 per cent of the population are students, 27 per cent are retired. Visitors and natives share the same basic pleasures – eating, drinking, chatting, promenading, people-watching and window shopping, all against a glorious backdrop of sun and sea. It's not difficult to fit in – all you have to do is enjoy yourself.

Having said that, life is just that bit easier if you observe some of the local niceties. Don't forget to say *bonjour* to the shopkeeper and *au revoir* when you leave the shop; include a *s'il vous plaît* when you ask for something and a *merci* when you receive it. Call the waiter '*monsieur*'. Begin a conversation with your hotel receptionist or bus driver with a few words of French, however bad; once local honour has been satisfied, you will soon find the conversation turns into English.

Hanging out, strolling, eating and drinking are major occupations

Culture

Whether it's due to the wealth and refined tastes of its upmarket 19th-century visitors or the magnetism that the Côte d'Azur has always exerted on artists, or maybe in an attempt to demonstrate that it's more than just a great holiday resort, Nice and its environs offer an amazing number of top-class public art galleries and museums. If you're serious about art (particularly 20th-century art), you could spend four or five days taking them all in. A pass giving unlimited access for any seven days within a period of 15 days to all of Nice's municipal galleries and museums (excluding the Chagall and Asiatic Art museums) can be purchased at any of them, price €6. If you're a frequent visitor to Nice, opt for a pass valid for 15 museum visits, to be used within one year, priced at €18.30. In any case, admission to all the municipal museums is free on the first and third Sundays of each month.

The cream of the 20th-century selection includes the Musée Matisse in the Cimiez district (see pages 99–100), the Musée national Message Biblique Marc Chagall just north of the city centre (see pages 100–1), MAMAC (Musée d'Art Moderne et d'Art Contemporain) near the Old Town, featuring a wide selection of international modern art (see page 98). Further afield, the Fondation Maeght at St-Paul-de-Vence (see page 136) is a treasure-house of over 6,000 works by Braque, Chagall, Léger, Kandinsky, Miró and others (although not all are on exhibit at the same time), while the Musée Renoir (ⓐ Chemin des Collettes ⓣ 04 93 20 61 07) at Cagnes preserves the artist's studio as it was in the last days of his life. More wide-ranging collections are housed in the Musée des Beaux-Arts

● *Musée Matisse is one of Nice's cultural highlights*

Jules-Chéret (see page 85), with priceless works of the 15th–20th centuries, and the Musée Masséna (if it ever reopens – see page 82), both to the west of the city centre.

Visitors with an interest in history and archaeology will want to see the Roman-era discoveries in the Musée d'Archéologique in Cimiez (see page 98) and the nearby Arènes (see pages 92–4), the prehistoric finds and reconstructions at Terra Amata (see page 101), and – when it finally reopens – the history of the city catalogued in the Musée Masséna. More specialist and farther out of town, but well worth a visit for the quality of its collections of oriental exhibits, is the Musée des Arts Asiatiques (see page 84).

The other main aspect of Nice's cultural life is music. Aside from the Jazz Festival (see page 106) or Musicalia (see page 20), the summer months are rich in musical events, many of them free: June has its sacred music recitals in churches around the town, and in July a series of free concerts of Mediterranean and world music, under the collective name **Musicalia**, takes place at the open-air Théâtre de Verdure near the seafront on Wednesday and Saturday evenings. The same venue sees performances of opera and operetta in September, as does the Opéra de Nice (see page 76). The What's On section of the Nice Tourism site (ⓦ www.nicetourism.com) gives listings and offers an on-line booking service for musical events.

◗ *Nice's outdoor activities are endless*

Shopping

SHOPPING AREAS & MARKETS

The few large department stores in Nice are found along av. Jean Médecin, including the unmissable ochre façade of Galeries Lafayette, a branch of the renowned Parisian store, and two blocks further up the Etoile shopping mall (four floors of chain-store fashion shops), cafés, FNAC and a large branch of C&A. The avenue also sports a wide range of smaller fashion boutiques and businesses selling bags and leatherware. Note: the construction of the new tramway (see page 57), running down av. Jean Médecin towards the sea, is due to be completed by the beginning of 2008.

The long, busy, pedestrianised zone of the rue de France and rue Masséna, heading west from the top of place Masséna, is a bustling thoroughfare of small souvenir shops and individual fashion boutiques. Famous designer names congregate just to the south and west of place Masséna, near the Jardin Albert 1er, and heading back towards rue Alphonse Karr and rue Paradis.

As well as containing the city's most enticing markets (see below), the Old Town is crowded with small shops. Many of them are true specialists in everything from faïence and mosaics to hand-made toiletries, chocolates and foodstuffs; others offer a general range of souvenirs aimed unashamedly at the tourist purse.

The markets in the cours Saleya in the Vieille Ville are great places to browse. In the daily flower and produce market (see page 66) you can pick up dried flowers, enticing packs of herbs and spices and craft items, as well as improbably coloured candy and sweets and top-quality fresh produce for a picnic. The night market in the same

● *The Marché aux Fleurs takes place on the Cours Saleya*

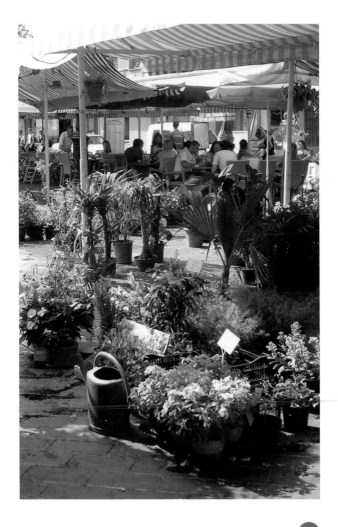

location (late spring to early autumn only) offers a wide range of gift ideas, from the funky to the irresistibly tacky. On Mondays the market changes to *brocante* (bric-a-brac): goods on sale range from exquisite vases to battered but authentic *gendarme*'s caps (as well as a lot of absolute junk).

BEST BUYS & LOCAL SPECIALITIES

There are no heart-stopping bargains in Nice but, equally, commerce is too competitive to allow rip-off prices. Generally, the quality is good for the price, and in some categories it can be very good indeed. Nice's proximity to the perfumeries of Grasse and herb-growing areas of Provence ensures a wide offering of hand-made perfumes, soaps and toiletries. Dried and fresh herbs are available in profusion and make

USEFUL SHOPPING PHRASES

What time do the shops open/close?
A quelle heure ouvrent/ferment les magasins?
Ah kehlur oovr/fehrm leh mahgazhang?

How much is this?
C'est combien?
Cey combyahng?

Can I try this on?
Puis-je essayer ceci?
Pweezh ehssayeh cerssee?

My size is ...
Ma taille (clothes)/
ma pointure (shoes) est ...
Mah tie/mah pooahngtewr ay ...

I'll take this one, thank you
Je prends celui-ci/celle-ci merci
*Zher prahng serlweesi/
sehlsee mehrsee*

good gifts in themselves. Olives and olive oil are another regional speciality, and Nice offers a tempting choice at a standard unmatched elsewhere on the Med (see specialist Oliviera, page 71). Colourful Provençal fabrics are sold everywhere, either by the length or made up as table linen or clothing. If you are seriously interested in antiques, the shops of the Quartier des Antiquaires (see page 72) are worth checking out, in addition to the Monday market in the cours Saleya (see left).

FOOD & EVERYDAY SHOPPING

As in most French cities, you are never far from a small grocer's shop or *boulangerie* (baker's), and of course the markets offer superb produce. If you need to buy a range of everyday necessities it makes sense to use one of the small supermarkets – look for the names Monoprix (central, on av. Jean Médecin), Casino and Intermarché (outlets along the blvd Gambetta on the western edge of the city centre and dotted regularly throughout the rest of the city). If you're travelling by car, the 140 stores of the Cap 3000 complex at St-Laurent-du-Var near the airport will satisfy your every shopping need.

⬤ *Printed Provençal fabrics make great take-home gifts*

Eating & drinking

WHERE TO GO

You will never have trouble finding somewhere to eat in Nice. Even late in the evening on Bastille Day you'd be unlucky to have to walk more than a few yards before coming across a free table for two. Budget is not a limitation, either: Nice caters equally well for cheap snacks and gourmet dining, with an endless mass of mid-range eateries in between that all offer a uniform but reliable bill of fare – excellent pizzas, standard pasta and Italian dishes, *moules frites* (steamed mussels and french fries) and seafood. Restaurants cluster around the main focal points of tourist traffic: the rue de France/rue Masséna pedestrian zone, the Vieille Ville, the seafront and the streets around the railway station. Don't overlook the port area, which is lined with excellent seafood restaurants and some lively bars. Oriental and Asian cuisine is well catered for in most of these areas, and Turkish and Middle Eastern establishments are not hard to find. Specifically vegetarian restaurants are few (see page 75 for one of the best, La Zucca Magica), but it's easy to find tasty meat- and fish-free pizzas and salads on any menu; higher-class establishments will nearly always offer vegetarian choices.

PRICE CATEGORIES

Based on the average cost of a three-course evening meal for one person, excluding drinks. Lunch will usually be cheaper, especially if you opt for the good-value *prix fixe* (set menu) option at lunchtime.

£ up to €20   ££ €21–50   £££ over €50

● *Le Bistrot de la Réserve serves up gourmet food with sea views*

Choosing a restaurant a few minutes' walk away from the most crowded streets will usually knock a few euros off the bill, though the ambience may not be so vibrant. Seafood, plentiful and top quality everywhere, is generally more expensive than meat-based dishes. The higher-range restaurants tend to close earlier, by 22.30 or 23.00, but the mid-range pizza/pasta eateries in the main tourist locations will still be serving (and still crowded) well after midnight.

A half-pint of beer (*une pression*) will set you back about €3, more if the bar or café is upmarket enough to set out a few complimentary olives and peanuts with your glass. On the other hand, you can make one drink last all night without getting a sour look from the waiter – drinking is regarded as an accompaniment to conversation, not an end in itself. If cocktails are your tipple, use the bar of a smart hotel; the versions served in ordinary cafés can be poor imitations. Most restaurants will offer a selection of mainly French wines; the climate and cuisine are tailor-made for a chilled bottle or carafe of rosé, in which the local Provençal and Corsican vineyards excel.

Restaurant menus are usually *service compris*, but if you have had really good service in a restaurant, leave a few euros, at your discretion (ten per cent is considered very generous). Again, it's common courtesy to leave the small change behind after a drink in a café. Major credit cards are accepted pretty much everywhere, but you may need to spend a minimum (usually €15) to use them. The French smoking ban comes into effect in February 2008, meaning that all bars and restaurants will be non-smoking, or must have a regulated, and very separate, smoking area.

FAST FOOD, LIGHT MEALS, PICNICS & SELF-CATERING

Nice has its own native fast-food options in *socca*, *pan bagnat* and *pissaladière* (see page 30), and you shouldn't leave without trying them. Take-away food in the shape of sandwiches, filled rolls, pizza slices and kebabs is ubiquitous.

Additionally, Nice is picnic heaven – fresh bread (and tempting pastries) from the *boulangerie*, cooked meats and cheese from the *charcuterie* and superb salads and fruit from the greengrocer's, or better still the morning market in the cours Saleya. Head to Place Gautier, a central square opening out on the north side of the *cours*, to buy divine seasonal produce, as well as jams, cheeses and *tapenade* (a type of olive pâté) directly from local farmers.

▶ *Everything for a picnic, for sale at the* boulangerie

● Salade niçoise *with all the trimmings*

LOCAL SPECIALITIES

Nice's best known dish is *salade niçoise*, a delicious summer option of tuna, eggs, anchovies, tomatoes and salad – the better the restaurant, the more elaborate the version. Served up in a roll as fast food it becomes *pan bagnat*. *Socca* is a simple snack consisting of an oven-baked pancake of chickpea flour and olive oil. *Pissaladière* is a thin pizza-like street food topped with fried onions, anchovies and olives (no cheese or tomato). If you want to try *bouillabaisse*, the south coast's traditional meal-sized fish stew, you'll need to find a restaurant that serves it, and even then you may be required to give up to 24 hours' notice.

USEFUL DINING PHRASES

I would like a table for ... people
Je voudrais une table pour ... personnes
Zher voodray ewn tabl poor ... pehrson

Waiter/waitress!
Monsieur/Mademoiselle,
s'il vous plaît!
*M'sewr/madmwahzel,
sylvooplay!*

May I have the bill, please?
L'addition, s'il vous plaît!
Laddyssyawng, sylvooplay!

Could I have it well-cooked/medium/rare please?
Je le voudrais bien cuit/à point/saignant
Zher ler voodray beeang kwee/ah pwang/saynyang

I am a vegetarian. Does this contain meat?
Je suis végétarien (végétarienne). Est-ce que ce plat
contient de la viande?
*Zher swee vehzhehtarianhg (vehzhehtarien). Essker ser plah
kontyang der lah veeahngd?*

Where is the toilet (restroom) please?
Où sont les toilettes, s'il vous plaît?
Oo sawng leh twahlaitt, sylvooplay?

Entertainment & nightlife

Nice's climate encourages open-air amusement. Enjoying a leisurely outdoor meal, relaxing with a drink or two, attending one of the open-air musical events such as the Jazz Festival or Musicalia (see page 20), taking in the night views over the Baie des Anges, the bustle of promenaders on the seafront, the antics of the street performers and the strains of the (mainly Eastern European) street musicians – for most visitors this is enough to fill an evening. However, the city offers plenty more active options.

CINEMA
You can catch movies in English (with French subtitles) at these cinemas:
Cinéma Rialto ⓐ 4 rue de Rivoli ⓣ 04 93 88 08 41, or recorded

CASINOS
If you're over 21 and can afford to lose a few euros, a casino provides great evening entertainment. Dress smartly to get past the doormen and take your passport with you for ID and then, after maybe playing a few of the slots, move on to the tables, for which there will be a small admission charge. You don't have to bet your shirt to enjoy the experience – the real entertainment is in watching the high rollers and rubbing shoulders with the Riviera's rich and (sometimes) famous. The serious action doesn't start until around 22.00, but you can pass the time in the bar or restaurant beforehand. Nice's two casinos, Casino Ruhl and Palais de la Méditerranée, are both on the promenade des Anglais (see pages 81–2 and 91).

🔺 *No one goes to bed early in Nice*

information 0892 680 041 Ⓝ Bus: 3, 7, 8, 9, 10, 14, 22, 52, 59, 94 200
Cinémathèque de Nice (see page 96) ⓐ 3 espl. Kennedy
ⓣ 04 92 04 06 66 Ⓝ Bus: 3, 4, 5, 6, 89, 116
Le Mercury ⓐ 16 pl. Garibaldi ⓣ 04 93 55 37 81, or recorded
information 0892 892 892

CLUBS, DISCOS & LIVE MUSIC

If your night isn't complete without dancing, there are plenty of
discos and bars where you can get your fix, from clubs and piano
bars to pubs and cafés with live music. Streets running off the
seafront, the Old Town and the port area are the best areas to check
out. See ⓦ www.nicetourism.com or the media listed on page 152.

Sport & relaxation

BEACH & WATERSPORTS

There are 15 beaches along the Baie des Anges, public beaches as well as the private stretches reserved for guests of hotels. All of them are pebble beaches, which doesn't put off the thousands of sun-worshippers every day. Beaches that feature a children's play area include Bambou, Forum, Lido, Miami, Neptune, Ruhl and Voilier. Bambou, Florida, Neptune and Voilier also have pedaloes for hire. If you like sand with your sea, take a short trip to neighbouring Villefranche-sur-Mer (see page 112) for a family-style beach or Beaulieu-sur-Mer (see page 121) for a more sedate resort.

Swimming is okay anywhere; the beaches get high EU ratings and are supervised by lifeguards, and the water reaches a very warm 25°C/77°F in summer. You'll be able to find opportunities to pursue a wide variety of watersports on Nice's beaches.

Jet skiing: Beau Rivage, Florida, Forum and Sporting

Parascending: Blue Beach, Forum, Neptune, Opera and Ruhl

Scuba diving: Nice is where much of today's standard scuba equipment was invented, by the Forjon family between the wars; the Centre International Plongée Raymond Lefevre offers a first-time for beginners (called a *baptême*) and packages for more experienced divers. ❸ 2 ruelle des Moulins, on the quai des 2 Emmanuel (in front of the Brasserie La Goelette,

🔺 *Birds-eye view of the Med*

on the east of the old port) ☎ 04 93 55 59 50 Ⓦ www.cip-nice.com
Villefranche is another good centre for diving of all kinds.

OTHER OUTDOOR ACTIVITIES

There are plenty of companies offering activities such as riding,
golf and hiking, but they all involve going some way out of town.
The Tourist Office (see page 152) will be happy to help you, and you
can preview the range of opportunities on the Around Nice (Sports)
section of Ⓦ www.nicetourism.com.

However, you don't have to go very far to enjoy walking. The hill
of Le Château (see pages 64–6) is perfect for a gentle stroll in the
fresh air. For a longer and more invigorating walk, catch a bus to the
hillside of Mont Boron (see pages 94–5).

SPORT

Nice's football (soccer) team plays at the 18,000-seater Stade du Ray
in the northern suburbs (Ⓐ Av. du Ray Ⓝ Bus: 1 or 18 from the city
centre). OGC Nice may not have the international presence of Riviera
neighbours AS Monaco, but in recent seasons they have managed a
respectable middle-league position in the French First Division. The
French football season runs from August to May, with most matches
played on Wednesdays and Saturdays. Crowds are small (12,000 for the
local derby with Monaco) but the supporters' Gallic passion makes
for a great atmosphere, and tickets are much cheaper than for English
Premiership games. See Ⓦ www.ogcnice.com for further information.

You can play *boules* (*pétanque*) on the beaches in Nice; at St-Paul-
de-Vence (see page 132) the local tourist office will sell you a package
of two hours of instruction. To see the experts at play, visit in July,
when Nice hosts the Europétanque d'Azur championships around
the Jardin Albert 1er, in which over 500 local teams participate.

Accommodation

With over 12,000 hotel beds and more than 700 holiday apartments, plus a good selection of youth hostels, Nice has no shortage of accommodation, although much of it is at the more expensive end of the market. The cheapest hotels cluster around the main railway station, which entails a bus ride or a 20-minute walk to the sea and the Old Town; mid-price options are mainly located in the central boulevards, a reasonable walk from the seafront, shops and sights. The central seafront and its side-streets are mostly the preserve of luxury hotels. If you're travelling by car, you also have the option of a reasonably priced motel room near the airport. Whatever accommodation you have in mind, remember that the French take their summer holidays in late July and August: book well in advance for that period.

HOTELS

Unless you have booked an inclusive package, it pays to investigate thoroughly on the web; in addition to the many commercial sites, the tourist office offers listings and instant reservations at Ⓦ www.niceres.com, which also covers self-catering options. Listed below are a few recommendations, but there are many more good hotels to choose from.

PRICE CATEGORIES

Based on the average cost of a double room. Breakfast is always extra and often poor value; some hotels lay on a full buffet, others the bare minimum of coffee, juice and rolls. If your hotel is one of the latter, take your *petit déjeuner* at any pavement café.
£ up to €100   ££ €100–200   £££ over €200

Hôtel Villa La Tour £ Hidden away on one of the Old Town's back streets near the flower market, this small hotel with 14 rooms oozes charm. **ⓐ** 4 rue de la Tour **ⓣ** 04 93 80 08 15 **ⓦ** www.villa-la-tour.com **ⓝ** Bus: 5-min walk from *gare routière*

Albert 1er £–££ A 1930s building on the edge of the Vieille Ville, with great views of the city and the bay. The 72 sound-proofed rooms have lovely oak furniture. **ⓐ** 4 av. des Phocéens **ⓣ** 04 93 85 74 01 **ⓦ** www.hotel-albert-1er.fr **ⓝ** Bus: 11, 52, 59, 60, 62, 98, 212

La Maison du Séminaire £–££ A former monastery to the east of Nice's port with fabulous sea-facing rooms. There's a fresco-filled chapel and a library with an unusual selection of world texts. **ⓐ** 29 blvd Franck Pilatte **ⓣ** 04 93 89 39 57 **ⓦ** www.maison-du-seminaire.com **ⓝ** Bus: 20, 30

Hôtel Suisse ££ Set into the cliffside of the Château hill at the eastern end of the Baie des Anges and well placed for the Vieille Ville and the port. There are staggering sea views from 35 of its 42 rooms. **ⓐ** 15 quai Rauba Capéu **ⓣ** 04 92 17 39 00 **ⓦ** www.hotels-ocre-azur.com **ⓝ** Bus: 15-min walk from *gare routière*

Villa Victoria ££ Central quiet location and helpful staff, with a shady garden for relaxation. **ⓐ** 33 blvd Victor Hugo **ⓣ** 04 93 88 39 60 **ⓦ** www.villa-victoria.com **ⓝ** Bus: 3, 7, 8, 9, 10, 14, 22, 38

Hôtel Windsor ££ This hotel is stylish and unique without costing a fortune. Many of the rooms have been individually decorated by leading contemporary artists. **ⓐ** 11 rue Dalpozzo **ⓣ** 04 93 88 59 35 **ⓦ** www.hotelwindsornice.com **ⓝ** Bus: 3, 7, 8, 9, 10, 14, 22, 52, 59, 94, 200, 400, 500, 710, 720, 750

● *Villa Victoria, one of many 19th-century town houses conversions*

Le Grimaldi ££–£££ Located near Nice's *zone piétonne* and main shopping areas, the Grimaldi is a comfortable choice for an indulgent city break. ● 15 rue Grimaldi ● 04 93 16 00 24 ● www.le-grimaldi.com ● Bus: 3, 7, 8, 9, 10, 14, 22, 52, 59, 94, 200, 400, 500, 710, 720, 750

Hôtel et Plage Beau Rivage ££–£££ Renovated a few years back by architect Jean-Michel Wilmotte, Old Town's Beau Rivage was Matisse's home between 1917 and 1918. Just steps away from the flower market and the seafront, the hotel boasts 118 rooms and a private beach. ● 24 rue St-François-de-Paule ● 04 92 47 82 82 ● www.hotel-beau-rivage-nice.cote.azur.fr ● Bus: 11, 52, 59, 60, 62

Hôtel Negresco £££ A Nice landmark since 1912 and the grand old lady of the Riviera, patronised over the years by the elite. All 121 rooms and 24 suites are lavishly and individually decorated, while the restaurant, Le Chantecler, is Michelin-starred (of course). ● 37 prom.

des Anglais ☎ 04 93 16 64 00 ⓦ www.hotel-negresco-nice.com
Ⓝ Bus: 11, 52, 59, 60, 62, 94, 98, 200, 400, 500, 710, 720, 790

Palais de la Méditerranée £££ The modern hotel and casino behind
the 1930 art deco façade of its predecessor was reopened in 2004.
Check out the gorgeous views from the sun terrace. ⓐ 15 prom. des
Anglais ☎ 04 92 14 77 00 ⓦ www.concorde-hotels.com Ⓝ Bus: 11, 52,
59, 60, 62, 94, 98, 200, 400, 500, 710, 720, 790

SELF-CATERING

For stays of a week or more, especially if travelling as a family, consider
renting a holiday apartment; many of the complexes are modern and
very central, and the abundance of food outlets and markets makes
self-catering easy. Prices often beat most mid-range hotels. Check out
the Nice tourism website (ⓦ www.nicetourism.com) for the options.

HOSTELS

Auberge de Jeunesse (HI) £ This youth hostel, located on a hillside
4 km/2½ miles out of town, has exceptional city views. It's open
from April to September and is by far the cheapest accommodation
option. ⓐ rte Forestière du Mont Alban ☎ 04 93 89 23 64
ⓦ www.hihostels.com Ⓝ Bus: 14, 82 to Route Forestière

Nice Camélias (HI) £ Basic rooms perfectly positioned in Nice's
bustling centre, equidistant from the city's main train station
and the Old Town. ⓐ 3 rue Spitalieri ☎ 04 93 62 15 54
ⓦ www.hihostels.com Ⓝ Bus: 4, 17, 18, 22

Villa Saint-Exupéry £ Although 3 km (2 miles) from Nice's centre, the
Villa more than makes up for its location with its leafy terraces, bar,

MAKING THE MOST OF NICE

THE NEGRESCO

Henri Negresco, Romanian-born director of the Monte Carlo Casino, decided he could trade on his excellent contacts with royalty and millionaires by creating the grandest hotel on the Riviera, a palace fit to house his superstar friends. The result was the 1912 pink and white confection by Edouard Niermans that has become a National Historic Building and an icon of Nice. The interior has a fabulous art collection, with some quirky touches, such as the carousel in the lobby and the gloriously tacky illuminated name sign outside. Unlike many of the world's big-name hotels, it is still privately owned and run.

huge self-catering kitchen, free breakfast and internet. Undoubtedly the best budget option around. ➋ 22 av. Gravier ❶ 04 93 84 42 83 ⓦ www.vsaint.com ⓝ Bus: 1, 2, 23

CAMPING

The Nice tourist office lists some 21 campsites. There are none in Nice itself; the nearest location is Cagnes-sur-Mer, about 20 km (12 miles) from the centre of Nice via the A8 motorway. ⓝ 30 mins by bus 94, 200, 400, or 500; less than 20 mins by train (bear in mind that the campsite may be some way from the bus stops and railway station in the middle of Cagnes). Other possibilities, a little further out, are Villeneuve-Loubet and Antibes. A local favourite is Camping Les Romarins (ⓦ www.campingromarins.com) at Eze, perched above Cap-Ferrat, with spectacular views.

● *The grand old lady has become a Nice landmark*

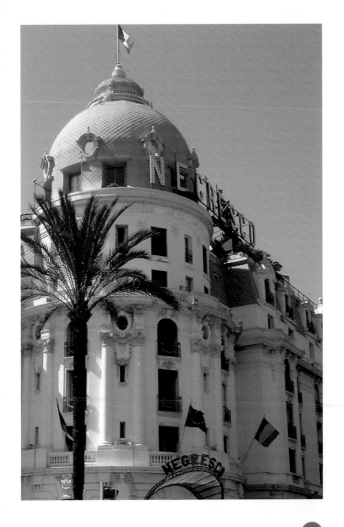

THE BEST OF NICE

Le Grand Tour These open-top bus tours last about 1½ hours and take in Cimiez to the north and Mont Boron in the east. Hop on and off the bus as often as you wish. Tickets are available on the bus or from tourist offices. The fare for a one-day pass is €18, a two-day pass is €21; there are reductions for children and seniors. ☎ 04 92 29 17 00 🕐 09.30–18.50 (last tour of the day, which is cheaper) Ⓝ Bus: 11, 52, 59, 60, 62, 98, 212

Petit Train Touristique A 40-minute tour, with commentary, of the Old Town and the Château hill. Fare €6.50, €3 for children under 9. Ⓦ www.petittrainnice.com 🕐 10.00–17.00 Jan–Mar; 10.00–18.00 Apr & May, Sept–Dec; 10.00–19.00 June–Aug; closed mid Nov–late Dec & early Jan–last weekend of Jan; departures every 30 mins. Ⓝ Bus: 11, 52, 59, 60, 62, 98, 212

For the best attractions for children, see pages 147–8.

TOP 10 ATTRACTIONS

- **Vieille Ville** Exploring the colourful streets and markets (see page 62).

- **Cathédrale Orthodoxe Russe St-Nicolas** The architecture and atmosphere of the Russian cathedral (see pages 78–81).

🔽 *Chaises longues along the beachfront*

- **Promenades** A summer evening stroll along the promenade des Anglais and quai des Etats-Unis. You're guaranteed a couple of hours of free entertainment.

- **A meal in the Cours Saleya** A leisurely outdoor dinner anywhere in the cours (see page 66) – enjoy the food and the buzz around you.

- **Musée Chagall** The famous artist's enigmatic masterpieces in Cimiez (see page 100).

- **A walk around the Château hill** (see pages 64–6) to cool off and admire the views of the Old Town and port. Collect your picnic ingredients in the market on the way there.

- **The Riviera** A day trip to any of the destinations listed on pages 108–9.

- **Open-air music** Jazz or classical music at the Arènes de Cimiez (see pages 92–4 and 106) or one of the free concerts of the Musicalia (page 20).

- **Lunch at the Negresco** A spoil-yourself treat at the Michelin-starred brasserie (see pages 38–40 and 81–2).

- **The Port by night** Soaking up the lively atmosphere or dancing the night away in one of the quayside bars.

Suggested itineraries

Here's a quick guide to seeing the best of Nice, depending on the time you have available.

HALF-DAY: NICE IN A HURRY

If you're just calling into Nice on a longer Riviera holiday, or maybe catching some sightseeing during a business trip, concentrate on the Vieille Ville (page 62). Try to make it a morning, so that you can experience the flower and produce market in the cours Saleya (not on Mondays) before heading up the side-streets and reaching the pl. Rossetti for a visit to the cathedral and a well-earned drink or ice cream at Fenocchio's. Don't miss the House of Adam and Eve, the Chapelle Ste-Rita or the Palais Lascaris on the way.

1 DAY: TIME TO SEE A LITTLE MORE

If you have the afternoon and early evening as well, leave the Old Town at the Ponchettes exit from cours Saleya and take a walk along the seafront, beginning along the quai des Etats-Unis and continuing along the promenade des Anglais as far as the Hôtel Negresco. You could use some of the time to soak up the sun on the beach, or head up from the promenade into the pedestrian-only rue Masséna for some retail therapy or a meal at one of the area's excellent pizza and pasta restaurants.

2–3 DAYS: TIME TO SEE MUCH MORE

After the above whistlestop tour of the centre, relax the next day with a morning stroll on the Château hill and descend from there into the port to marvel at the opulent yachts and enjoy some freshly caught seafood. From the port it's not a long walk to MAMAC (see page 98) and its quirky pop-art collection. Use your remaining time for short bus rides to Cimiez for the Chagall and Matisse museums, the Roman remains and the Franciscan monastery (see pages 98–100), to the Russian Orthodox cathedral in the northwest of the town (see pages 78–81), and a little further afield, to the Beaux-Arts or Asiatic Art museums (see pages 84–5).

LONGER: ENJOYING NICE TO THE FULL

You'll want to return to some of the places suggested in the 2–3 day schedule, by day and night, but a longer visit gives you time to explore other places along the Riviera, which is easy with the excellent train and bus services. Make Villefranche (page 112) and St-Paul-de-Vence (page 132) your top priorities.

● You can catch the flower market on any day except Monday

Something for nothing

You don't have to put your credit card into the red to enjoy Nice, and many of its best experiences come at little or no charge. A cup of coffee at an outside table may seem a little pricey in itself, but it buys you a seat all morning if you want, while passing performance artists, locals and tourists keep you constantly entertained. Sunshine, fabulous views and fresh air are free, and there's nowhere better to enjoy them than the Château park (see pages 64–6). If you get too hot, stand close to the waterfall and let it spray you cool.

It costs nothing to walk along the seafront in the evening and take in the street life – from seriously competitive rollerbladers to African drumming groups – that the promenade and the beach attract like magnets. In fact, anywhere in central Nice is good for people-watching, especially the markets. Browsing antiques at the Monday morning market in the cours Saleya is an enjoyable experience that costs nothing, and even if you decide to buy something, the process of haggling with the vendor brings its own free show into the bargain, as the entire gamut of human emotion and Gallic gesture are displayed.

Remember that all the municipal museums (except the Chagall and Asiatic Art museums) have free entrance on the first and third Sundays of each month. Other must-see sights that are permanently free of charge include the cathedral (pages 78–81) and the Palais Lascaris (page 68). You can enjoy Musicalia, free concerts of Mediterranean and world music, at the open-air Théâtre de Verdure (between the seafront and the Jardin Albert 1er) on Wednesday and Saturday evenings in July.

▶ *People-watching all morning for the price of a cup of coffee*

When it rains

You'd be unlucky, even in winter, to be forced indoors by rain in Nice
for more than a morning, but for days when even the Mediterranean
looks grey, the city offers all kinds of escapes.

With over 60 museums and galleries in the vicinity, not to mention
villas, churches and palaces, there's always somewhere to while
away a few hours indoors. The star museums – Musée Chagall,
Musée Matisse, MAMAC, the Beaux-Arts and Asiatic Arts museums
– could all easily occupy a half day. If you're a cinema buff you'll love
the Cinémathèque's performances of old classics in all languages
(see page 96). Bad weather can't spoil the indoor attractions of the
Old Town either – its baroque churches, the cathedral, the Palais
Lascaris – and it also provides the perfect opportunity to gaze at the
bejewelled interior of the Russian Orthodox Cathedral.

As well as cultural attractions, the temples of commerce offer a very
handy refuge from the weather. Browsing in the Galeries Lafayette or
the Etoile shopping mall on av. Jean Médecin could keep shopaholics
happily occupied for an entire day, if you include a spot of lunch.
Smaller shops also have more to offer than you think – several of
the mosaics boutiques in the Vieille Ville invite you to try your hand
at this fascinating handicraft. In the same area, Poterie Painting
(see page 72) will show you how to create your own souvenirs by
designing and painting your own pottery to take away with you.
If you're looking for something more active, why not get wet anyway,
in one of Nice's indoor swimming pools? The two most central are:

Piscine Jean Médecin 🄰 178 rue de France 🅃 04 93 86 24 01 🄽 Bus: 3, 8, 9
Piscine St-François 🄸 13 pl. St-François 🅃 04 93 85 53 08

▶ *Browsing in galleries is a great way to escape the rain*

On arrival

TIME DIFFERENCE

French clocks follow Central European Time (CET). During Daylight Saving Time (end Mar–end Oct), the clocks go forward one hour.

ARRIVING

By air

The descent to Nice by air is an experience in itself. The runways are almost surrounded by the sea, and as the plane comes in to land you get some wonderful views of the Côte d'Azur. The airport is the second largest in France in terms of passengers (close to ten million a year), but it's a manageable size and gets its customers landside pretty quickly. In each of the two terminals there are two banks to take care of any foreign exchange needs, ● 08.00–22.00 all year. The airport isn't a long way from the city (just 7 km/4 miles). Buses run from outside Terminals 1 and 2 every half-hour and take about 30 minutes. (Bus 98 goes to the city's *gare routière*, or main bus station, and from mid-July to mid-September it also goes to the Port ● 06.00–23.45; Bus 99 goes to Nice-Ville, the city's main train station ● 06.00–21.00 Ⓦ www.lignedazur.com). Note that the €4 fare covers not only the bus trip, but is actually (an obligatory) day pass, valid on all Ligne d'Azur buses until midnight. If you prefer to take a taxi, the journey time is about the same and the fare around €30. For the same price you can pre-book a door-to-door minibus from Ⓦ www.a-t-s.net, though it's better value if there are 5–8 people in your party. The local TER train will get you to Nice-Ville station in about six minutes, but, strangely enough, there's no bus transfer that covers the 500-metre walk from the terminal to St Augustin, the airport station. Car hire firms at the airport include ADA, Avis, Budget, Europcar, Hertz, National/Alamo

🔺 *The views start before you even land*

and Sixt; the pick-up point is outside Terminal 2 (reached from Terminal 1 via a free shuttle bus).

Nice-Côte d'Azur Airport ❶ flight information 0820 423 333
ⓦ www.nice.aeroport.fr

By rail

The main SNCF railway station, Nice-Ville, is situated on the northern edge of the city centre, and is served by many buses (Bus 4 offers the most direct route to central Nice, and as of 2008, the city's new tram system will provide a direct link), as well as taxis. As in most large cities, the area near the station is not somewhere to linger at night, although Nice-Ville itself is safe and patrolled by uniformed security at all times.

Gare SNCF Nice-Ville ❷ av. Thiers ❶ information 04 92 14 82 52/53
ⓦ www.sncf.fr

By road

Long-distance and international buses arrive at Nice's *gare routière* (central bus station), which is conveniently located just north of the

Old Town and about ten minutes' walk to the centre of the city, from where you can catch a number of local buses to your onward destination. For help with planning journeys from Nice, ask at the information centre. ⓐ 5 blvd Jean Jaurès ⓣ 04 93 85 61 81

The A8 motorway skirts the northern edge of Nice. If approaching from the west, turn off at junction 50 either onto the *autoroute urbain sud*, the urban motorway, which will take you to the north of the centre, or follow signs to the promenade des Anglais to arrive at the seafront itself. Make sure you adjust quickly to slow-moving traffic and watch out for one-way systems as you approach the centre. It's a good idea to park as soon as you get near the centre. If you take the urban motorway, turn off towards 'Gare SNCF' and park at the av. Thiers car park; there is a tourist office at the nearby railway station. If you arrive on the promenade, the first central car park you will see is near the Musée Masséna, 200 yards from the city's main tourist office.

By water

Nice's commercial port offers frequent ferries to Corsica (Bastia, Calvi, Ile Rousse and Ajaccio). For information and timetables, check **Corsica Sardinia Ferries** (ⓦ www.corsicaferries.com) or **SNCM Ferries** (ⓦ www.sncm.fr). Both companies operate traditional slower car ferries (journey time approximately about five hours) and high-speed links (around three hours) to and from the island.

FINDING YOUR FEET

Once you've arrived, you'll find that the noise and traffic, though ever-present, are not as bad as in many Mediterranean cities. Although the only true pedestrian zones (*zones piétonnes*) are the Vieille Ville and the rue de France/rue Masséna, many of the boulevards see little traffic. The main arteries – promenade des

Anglais, av. Jean Médecin and the roads flanking the central Paillon green space – are always busy. It's okay to cross the street at any point if there's no traffic (but check that you know which way it should be coming – most of Nice's roads are one-way).

Check out the personal safety tips on pages 145–146, although you are unlikely to feel threatened in central Nice at any time. Pickpockets are the most likely danger you'll encounter – get into the habit of keeping your bag or purse closed and within sight. Bring a map with you or get one from a shop or the tourist office as soon as you can; asking directions can be frustrating when half the people you meet are strangers to Nice as well.

IF YOU GET LOST, TRY ...

Excuse me, do you speak English?
Excusez-moi, vous parlez anglais?
Ekskeweh mwah, voopahrlay ahnglay?

Excuse me, is this the right way to the Old Town/the city centre/the tourist office/the station/the bus station?
Excusez-moi, c'est la bonne direction pour la vieille ville/
le centre-ville/l'office de tourisme/la gare/la gare routière?
*Ekskewzaymwah, seh lah bon deerekseeawng poor lah veeay veel/
leh sahngtr veel/lohfeece de tooreezm/lah gahr/lah gahr rootyair?*

Can you point to it on my map?
Pourriez-vous me le montrer sur la carte?
Pooreehvoo mer ler mawngtreh sewr lah kart?

Nice

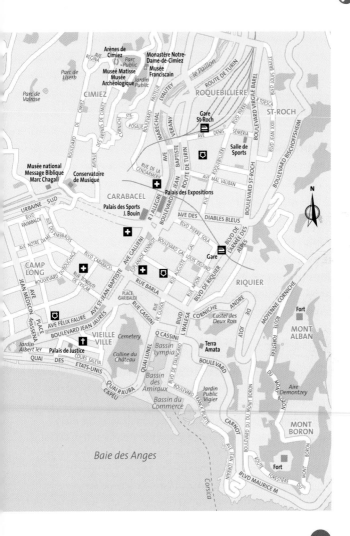

Parc de Valrose

Parc de Liserb

AVE REGINA

Arènes de Cimiez

Parc Public

Musée Matisse
Musée Archéologique

CIMIEZ

Monastère Notre-Dame-de-Cimiez

Musée Franciscain

le Paillon

ROUTE DE TURIN

Jardin Public

PASTEUR

VAUTEY

STE ROSALIE

CORNICHE

BOULEVARD DE CIMIEZ

AVENUE DES ARÈNES DE CIMIEZ

BOULEVARD VIRGILE BAREL

AVE LOUS BRAILLE

BOULEVARD PIERRE

AVE TOESCA

ROQUEBILLIÈRE

ST-ROCH

BOULEVARD JEAN XXIII

Gare St-Roch

AVE DENIS

SEMERIA

BOULEVARD BISCHOFFSHEIM

MARÉCHAL

VERANY

Salle de Sports

Musée national Message Biblique Marc Chagall

Conservatoire de Musique

RUE DE LA GENDARMERIE

AVE BAPTISTE

ROUTE DE TURIN

ROQUEBILLIÈRE

AVE MAL VAUBAN

BOULEVARD ST-ROCH

CARABACEL

Palais des Sports J. Bouin

Palais des Expositions

URBAINE SUD

BLVD RAIMBALDI

AVE NOTRE DAME

AVE ST-AMBROISE

BOULEVARD CARABACEL

R J ALLÈGRE

BOULEVARD JEAN

AVE DES

DIABLES BLEUS

BLVD PIERRE SOLA

BOULEVARD GALILOUE DELFINO

BLVD DE L'ARMÉE DES ALPES

Gare

CAMP LONG

BOULEVARD DU BOUCHAGE

AVE GALLIENI

RUE TONDUTI DE L'ESCARÈNE

AVE ST-JEAN-BAPTISTE

RUE BARLA

RUE PAINLEVÉ KENNEDY

RUE AUGUSTE

RUE ARSON

RUE DE RIQUIER

RIQUIER

AVE JEAN MEDECIN

PLACE MASSÉNA

AVE FÉLIX FAURE

RUE TONDUTI DE L'ESCAR

PLACE GARIBALDI

RUE CASSINI

RUE DE GUSOU

BLVD DE RIQUIER

CORNICHE ANDRÉ

DE JOLY

MOYENNE CORNICHE

ROUTE FORESTIÈRE

Fort

MONT ALBAN

Jardin Albert Ier

Palais de Justice

BOULEVARD JEAN JAURÈS

VIEILLE VILLE

COURS SALEYA

Cemetery

Colline du Château

Q CASSINI

L WALESA

Castel des Deux Rois

BLVD DE STALINGRAD

BOULEVARD DU MONT BORON

QUAI DES ÉTATS-UNIS

QUAI LUNEL

Bassin Olympia

Bassin des Amiraux

Terra Amata

BOULEVARD

Jardin Public Vigier

MONT BORON

QUAI RAUBA CAPEU

Bassin du Commerce

AVE MARC PARTE

CARNOT

Aire Demontzey

BOULEVARD DU MONT BORON

ROUTE

MONT BORON

Baie des Anges

Corsica

Fort

FORESTIÈRE

BLVD MAURICE M

N

Dress comfortably, and as casually as you like. However, the locals have a low tolerance of swimwear, and shirtless men, in the streets. Even the bus station displays a warning against 'unsuitable attire'. Save it for the beach or your hotel balcony. You'll notice that local girls always throw on a lightweight wrap as soon as they leave the beach.

ORIENTATION

The centre of Nice is defined by the west-to-east seafront (promenade des Anglais, becoming the quai des Etats-Unis further east), the north–south avenue Jean Médecin, and the wide boulevard-flanked spaces of the Paillon (Nice's river, now covered over with parks and squares in the centre) coming down from the northeast and meeting Jean Médecin at place Masséna before continuing to the promenade des Anglais as the Jardin Albert 1er. The west–east top of the walkable centre is formed by the blvd Victor Hugo, crossing Jean Médecin to become the blvd Dubouchage. The Italianate Old Town (Vieille Ville, also called Vieux Nice) is a triangular pocket of narrow streets and alleyways formed by the Paillon and the seafront, its third side being the green bulk of the Château hill. On the other side of the Château is the Port area. Between Jean Médecin, Victor Hugo and the promenade is the other main area of hotels, shops and restaurants, at its heart the pedestrian zone of rue de France and rue Masséna.

The maps in this book are up to date and show all the main sights and streets in each area, but many of the places that we list are on smaller streets. If you are planning to stay in Nice for longer than a couple of days, it's a good idea to acquire a detailed map, preferably one with a street index, from a local news-stand or bookshop or from the tourist office.

GETTING AROUND

It's no hardship to get around on foot in Nice – the entire length and breadth of the centre is no more than a 30–40-minute walk in any direction. For sights outside this area, you'll need to catch a bus or train.

Bus

Nice has an excellent bus system, day and night (night buses are called Noctambus), run by the regional company Ligne d'Azur (ⓦ www.lignedazur.com). A detailed bus map, which covers the city and most of the outlying places mentioned in this book, is obtainable from the tourist offices, but not, strangely, from the central bus station. All bus stops display their names, clear maps and timetables for the routes that serve them. The company also allows you to download a timetable for each of its routes from its website, which is worth doing if you have particular destinations in mind, as the help desk at the central bus station is not very generous with them.

A single journey anywhere in Nice (or along the Côte d'Azur) costs €1.30, payable to the driver on boarding (always board at the front). He can also sell you a one-day pass (€4 for unlimited travel by one person in one day), a seven-day pass (€15, unlimited travel by one person in seven consecutive days) or a multi-ticket (€20, which is good for 17 journeys and can be used by one or more people simultaneously). *Tabacs* (tobacconists' shops, which display a red diamond sign outside) sell ten-journey multi-tickets, too.

Nice is also busy building what is only the second tramway line in its history (the original 1880 line gave way to trolleybuses in 1953); it's scheduled to open at the beginning of 2008. When complete the tramway will provide a quick and easy way of navigating between the shops of avenue Jean Médecin, the central bus station and the Old Town.

Antibes, Marseille
& Paris

Nice
Ville

99

Aéroport

Thiers-
Gambetta

Poste
Thiers

St-Philippe

Thiers-
Gambetta

Gare
SNCF

99

Les
Potiers

Rossini

R. des
Baumettes

Frédéric Passy

Franklin

Franklin

Sevillan

Mozart

Les
Baumettes   38

Av. des
Fleurs

Alsace
Lorraine

Alphonse Karr

Av. des
Orangers

Guiglia

Dubouchage

Maeterlinck

Gambetta
Bottero

Verdi

Longchamp

Musée Chéret

Congrés
Joffre

Château des
Baumettes

Gambetta
Dante

Gambetta
Dante

Grosso C.U.M.

Grosso -
Centre Universitaire Méditerranéen

Grosso -
Centre Universitaire Méditerranéen

Aéroport   23

15   Rimiez   Destination &
Route Number

⚭   Interchange
with other lines

Service stops in
one direction only

Stop in both directions

Interchange at street level
(10-50 metre walk)

A Communicarta
Style **45** design
© Communicarta Ltd 2007 UDN.2
Map user Ref:WZFG/CS/NCE/07/15

98

Aéroport

Train

Local trains aren't much use to visitors for getting around within the city, but they are a great way to travel along the coast and into the mountains – see pages 108–9. If you're planning on visiting various locations on the same day, the €11 Carte Isabelle (available from Nice Ville Gare SNCF from 1 July to 30 September only) gives one day of unlimited travel on the regular trains between Cannes and the Italian border.

Taxis

Not a cheap option in Nice, especially at night (19.00–07.00), when the rates are higher. You can pick up a cab from ranks in front of the Negresco, on the promenade des Anglais av. Félix Faure, rue de l'Hôtel des Postes (at the back of Galeries Lafayette) or the main railway station. Otherwise call: **Central Taxi Riviera** 🕿 04 93 13 78 78 🕘 24 hours

Driving

The public car park underneath the flower market and Parking Infranet on the port are centrally located options. On-street parking is hard to find, but even if you do you can expect other drivers to park so close that you can't get away when you want to.

Car Hire

All of the major rental companies and many local ones have offices around the main railway station, Gare Nice-Ville ⓐ av. Thiers. (For airport car rentals, see pages 50–1). A comprehensive list of locations is available on the tourist office website. Many hotels can arrange car hire, and usually have the car brought to the hotel.

● *The Vieille Ville often looks more Italian in places than French*

THE CITY OF
Nice

Old Nice & the Port

The Château hill and the port below it was the site of the ancient
Greek settlement Nikaia. Later, the medieval town grew up to the
west in the triangle now known as the Vieille Ville (Old Town) or
Vieux Nice. This is a partly pedestrianised maze of narrow streets
opening out onto small squares, whose centre is the busy open
space of the cours Saleya, which adjoins the seafront of quai des
Etats-Unis at the old fish market buildings. Apart from one or two
municipal buildings, the look and feel of its colourful architecture is
pure Italy, with a dash of North African souk at the northeast end.

SIGHTS & ATTRACTIONS

Cathédrale de Ste-Réparate

North of the rue de la Poissonnerie the Old Town becomes a warren
of crowded but traffic-free alleys and streets. Follow the signs to
'Cathédrale' and you'll arrive in the place Rossetti, a lively mass
of café tables surrounding an 18th-century fountain, and Nice's
cathedral, dedicated to the third-century Palestinian martyr Saint
Réparata. The ornate plasterwork and bright colours, inside and out,
are the baroque style at its most Mediterranean; Ste-Réparate was

WHAT'S IN A NAME?
You will notice that, in deference to Nice's unique local identity,
most of the street names in the Vieille Ville are displayed in
both French and the local dialect Niçard or Nissart, a dying
language, which is currently kept alive by Nice's older generations.

Old Nice & the Port

Baie des Anges

QUARTIER DES ANTIQUAIRES

VIEILLE VILLE

Notre-Dame du Port

Palais Lascaris

Maison d'Adam et Eve

Chapelle Ste-Suaire

Colline du Château

Monument du Morts

Cathédrale de Ste-Réparate

Palais de la Préfecture

Église de Ste-Rita

Flower Market

Produce Market

Galerie de la Marine

Palais Rusca

Palais de Justice

Chapelle de la Miséricorde

Fish Market

Galerie des Ponchettes

Théâtre de Verdure

Lycée d'État Massena

Jardins Suspendus

Jardin Albert Ier

Espace Massena

Galeries Lafayette

PL MASSENA

Bassin du Commerce

Corsica

Bassin Lympia

Port du Plaisance

Bassin des Amiraux

Cemetery

	POI
	Cathedral
	Information
	Police Station
	Airport
	Railway Stn
	Bus Station
	Hospital

0 250 metres
0 250 yards

N

built between 1650 and 1757, replacing the original hilltop cathedral (see below). Don't miss the interior or the polychrome-tiled roof of the dome.

La Colline du Château

This commanding hill and public park was once the centre of power of the ancient Greek city of Nikaia and of the Dukes of Savoy, and was also the site of Nice's first cathedral of Ste-Marie, the ruins of which can still be seen at the top of the hill. The Château's fortifications were strong enough to withstand a combined Franco-Turkish siege in 1543; subsequent French assaults in 1691 and again in 1705 were more successful, and in 1706 Louis XIV ordered the demolition of the castle from which the hill takes its name. From 1783 the northern side began to be used as a burial ground – Catholic, Protestant and Jewish cemeteries still occupy this area – but in 1821 the city council had the happy idea of creating a public park, which was laid out in its present form after 1860.

Today the Château is a great place for strolling and taking in stunning views of the Old Town, the port and the sea. If you are the energetic type you can walk the steps leading from the end of the rue Rossetti, or take the easy way and use the *ascenseur* (lift) at the seafront end (€0.80 one way, €1.10 return). Atop the hill are several kilometres of easy walking paths, leading you to the ruins of the medieval cathedral, an orientation table and a cooling cascade facing the Vieille Ville, as well as a café and a children's playground. Note the interesting modern mosaics in pavements and steps on the eastern side. It's an easy walk down, either back to the Old Town or to the port.

Château lift ❸ End of the quai des Etats-Unis, near the Hôtel Suisse

▶ *The narrow streets of the Vieille Ville all seem to lead to the cathedral*

🕐 08.00–20.00, July & Aug; 08.00–19.00, May, June & Sept; 08.00–18.00, Oct–Apr

Cours Saleya

The rue St-François-de-Paule opens into this pedestrian area, the heart of the Old Town, which is thronged by visitors day and night. The colourful flower and produce market is held every day except Monday (produce during the morning only), accompanied by local craft stalls. Every square inch is reclaimed for restaurant tables as soon as the market departs. On Mondays the flowers give way to *brocante*, that useful French word covering everything from genuine antiques to junk. Two churches overlook the cours Saleya: the Chapelle de la Miséricorde of 1740, with a magnificent baroque interior, and at the very end, on the corner of rue Gilly, the gold-coloured façade of the Chapelle St-Suaire, built for the use of the 17th-century judicial body, the Sénat.

Palaces

Midway along, cours Saleya opens out onto the place Gautier, whose backdrop is the white Palais de la Préfecture, formerly the Palace of the Dukes of Savoy, built in the 17th century for use by the city's Italian rulers and now the seat of the Prefect of the Alpes-Maritimes *département*. Further along the rue Alexandre Mari from the Préfecture is the neo-classical Palais de Justice (law courts), dominating the wide place du Palais, where every doorway is adorned with lawyers' brass plaques. Across the square is the Palais Rusca, with its jolly pink clock tower.

The Port

Nice's port is home to some luxurious yachts in the marina (Port du Plaisance and Bassin Lympia), from where you can also

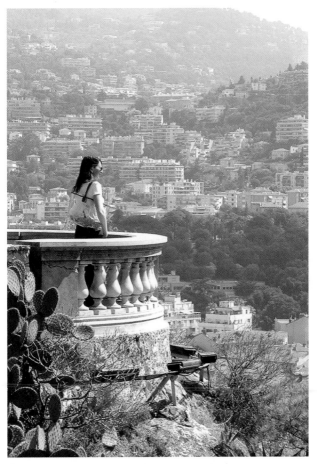

⬤ *The east side of the Château overlooks the Port and Mont Boron*

take day trips by boat to destinations such as Monaco, St-Tropez and the Ile Ste-Marguerite. A free shuttle bus will take you from any part of the quayside to the commercial port, which serves the giant car ferries to Corsica and Sardinia as well as the many Mediterranean cruise ships that call at Nice. The atmosphere of the Port de Plaisance is laid-back by day and night; the quaysides are where you'll find some of the best bars and seafood restaurants in Nice. From here it's an easy stroll back around the foot of the Château hill, passing Place Guynemer, along the quai Rauba Capéu and onto the main seafront of the quai des Etats-Unis. ⓦ Bus: 1, 2, 7, 9, 10, 14, 81, 100

Rue Droite

One of the most direct paths through the Old Town, the rue Droite (or 'straight road') comes out at the place St-François, where you'll see the old town hall and on Monday–Saturday mornings the tiny but lively fish market. En route it's easy to walk straight by the Palais Lascaris, a perfectly preserved aristocratic town house, which appears as little more than a doorway onto the street. Enter and discover the monumental staircase and upstairs staterooms housing art exhibitions, including material on loan from the (currently closed) Musée Masséna. Highlights are the decorated ceilings of the entrance hall, the recreated apothecary's shop just inside the door and the first-floor chapel, used for noble family weddings. Plans are currently underway to establish the Musée de la Musique de Nice (dedicated to traditional Niçois music) in the Palais as well.

Palais Lascaris ❷ 15 rue Droite ❶ 04 93 62 72 40 ❺ 10.00–18.00 Wed–Mon, closed Tues & some holidays

---

❶ *Shops and restaurants surround the Port de Plaisance*

Rue de la Poissonnerie

On the corner of this narrow street, heading north from the eastern end of cours Saleya, you can see the last remaining decorated house in the Vieille Ville, the Maison d'Adam et Eve, dating from the 16th century. Tucked away on the opposite side a little further up is the 17th-century Eglise de Ste-Rita (also known as the Chapelle de l'Annonciation), dedicated to the patron saint of hopeless cases; the restored interior is a baroque jewel.

Rue St-François-de-Paule

Enter the Vieille Ville from the Jardin Albert 1er along this shop-lined street, which takes its name from the 18th-century church of St Francis of Paola (a popular French–Italian Renaissance friar, now officially the patron saint of Italian fishermen) on the left. Almost opposite is the city's Opéra, an imposing 1885 imitation of Garnier's Paris opera house.

CULTURE

If you want a complete change from the Vieille Ville's stunning array of baroque churches, head for the seafront and check out the changing exhibitions of contemporary artists' work at the Galerie des Ponchettes and Galerie de la Marine. Alternately, head down the Old Town's rue Droite, where galleries compete for attention with eccentric paintings, unusual sculpture and a wide range of crafts.

Galerie de la Marine ⓐ 59 quai des Etats-Unis ⓣ 04 93 62 37 11 ⓛ 10.00–18.00, Tues–Sun, closed Mon

Galerie des Ponchettes ⓐ 77 quai des Etats-Unis ⓣ 04 93 62 31 24 ⓛ 10.00–18.00, Tues–Sun, closed Mon

RETAIL THERAPY

Aside from the flower and produce markets, from spring through autumn the cours Saleya has a colourful night market of gifts, crafts, toys and the like, which range from the desirable to the weird. On Mondays (🕑 08.00–18.00) the bric-a-brac market is worth browsing for antiques, militaria, craft items and old cast-offs. If you see something you really like and you've got the time, it's worth bargaining. The pl. du Palais hosts specialist markets on Saturdays between 08.00 and 18.00: second-hand books (1st & 3rd Sats); paintings and crafts (2nd Sat); old postcards (4th Sat).

The Vieille Ville itself is packed with shops, high-quality specialist boutiques mingling with mass-market outlets.

L'Atelier des Cigales With gorgeous items literally spilling out onto the street, this is the place to go for candles, knick-knacks and the finest and funkiest in hand-painted tableware. ⓐ 13 rue du Collet 🕿 04 93 85 70 62 🕑 10.30–19.30

L'Atelier des Jouets Follow the constant stream of bubbles to this corner shop, toys (many of them hand-made) of the highest quality. ⓐ 7 rue Gilly 🕿 04 93 13 09 60 🕑 10.30–19.00 Thur–Tues, 15.30–19.00 Wed

Oliviera For locally produced olive oil, head to Oliviera. Can't decide which type you'd like to take home? Stop for lunch or dinner, and a chance to taste owner Nadim's favourites, married with traditional Niçois dishes. ⓐ 2 rue Benoit Bunico 🕿 04 93 13 06 45 ⓦ www.oliviera.com 🕑 10.30–late Tues–Sat, 10.30–15.00 Sun & Mon

GOING CHEAP

The government strictly regulates Nice's twice-yearly sales periods, which usually occur around the beginning of January and the beginning of July. Hit the high-street shops around av. Jean Médecin for some of the best bargains.

Poterie Painting encourages you to create a truly unique souvenir by designing and painting your own pottery; your (or your children's) artistic efforts are then glazed and fired ready to take away. **a** 1 rue du Pont Vieux **t** 04 93 80 51 77 **c** 10.00–19.00

Quartier des Antiquaires is the place for real antique shops; in particular, the **Village Ségurane**, on the corner of rue Catherine Ségurane and rue Gautier, is a two-storey mall of quality antiques outlets. **a** Around rue Gautier, on the eastern side of the Château hill **b** Bus: 1, 2, 7, 9, 10, 14, 81, 100

TAKING A BREAK

The choice of cafés for a quick coffee or drink or a light lunch is limitless. The liveliest areas are the cours Saleya and the place Rossetti, which has the added attraction of Fenocchio, an ice cream paradise. *Socca* (see page 30), baguettes and other take-away snacks are ubiquitous, with a definite North African/Middle Eastern bias to the fare on offer where the rue Droite meets the place St-François. There's no shortage of pizzerias in the Old Town for a quick lunch, but a one-course seafood meal at one of the restaurants lining the port's quays can be surprisingly cheap.

● *Place Rossetti is a major hangout by day or night*

Chez René £ ❶ The classic place for *socca*. Order food at the bar and your drinks at one of the outside tables, then wait for the food to be served. ⓐ 2 rue Miralheti ❶ 04 93 92 05 73 ● 09.00–23.00 Tues–Sun

Confiserie Florian £ ❷ Stop by at Florian to watch 30 years of confectionery techniques in action, then pop upstairs for a taste of your favourites. ⓐ 14 quai Papacino ❶ 04 93 55 43 50 ⓦ www.confiseieflorian.com ● 10.00–19.00 Ⓝ Bus: 1, 2, 7, 9, 10, 14, 81

Fenocchio £ ❸ This long-established ice cream parlour offers more flavours than you'd have thought possible – and every single one of them is fabulous. ⓐ 2 pl. Rossetti ❶ 04 93 80 72 52 ● 10.00–24.00; closed Nov–Mar

La Fougasserie £ ❹ Head to this excellent Old Town *boulangerie* and take your pick of their tasty quiches – carrot, tuna and tomato or spinach and *chèvre* (goat's cheese) are just some of the choices on offer. ⓐ 5 rue de la Poissonerie ❶ 04 93 80 92 45

AFTER DARK

RESTAURANTS
Tartane £ ❺ Entirely off the beaten track, the Tartane is a home-style eatery with all the right stuff – the friendliest owners, the most fabulous pizza and giant jugs of chilled wine. All this, and at budget prices. ⓐ 44 blvd de Stalingrad ❶ 04 93 89 66 91 ● Mon–Sat

La Merenda ££ ❻ This tiny restaurant serving French cuisine may offer little in the way of ambience, but for true foodies, a stop at Le Merenda is essential. ⓐ 4 rue Raoul Bosio (marked on some maps

with the street's former name, rue de la Terrasse) ❶ No reservations
🕐 Mon–Fri

Tire-Bouchon ££ ❼ As a change from Italian and *Nissard* dishes,
sample the classic Lyonnais cuisine of this small restaurant just north
of the cours Saleya (booking advisable). ❷ 19 rue de la Préfecture
❶ 04 93 92 63 64 🕐 19.00–22.30

La Zucca Magica ££ ❽ 'The Magic Pumpkin' offers an entirely
vegetarian, scrumptious five-course set menu. ❷ 4 bis quai Papacino
❶ 04 93 56 25 27 🕐 12.30–14.30 & 19.30–22.30 Tues–Sat Ⓝ Bus: 1, 2, 7, 9

L'Ane Rouge £££ ❾ 'The Red Donkey' is a long-established Michelin-
starred restaurant on the eastern quay of the port: fine dining, leaning
to seafood and local specialities, at the sort of prices you'd expect.
Booking advisable. ❷ 7 quai des Deux Emmanuels ❶ 04 93 89 49 63
🕐 12.00–14.00, 19.00–22.00 Thur–Tues Ⓝ Bus: 1, 2, 7, 9, 10, 14, 81, 100

🔺 *Nice harbour by night*

Le Bistrot de la Réserve de Nice £££ ❿ Finnish chef Jouni Tormanen serves up an ever-changing menu of seasonal specialities, with a side of sea views to die for. Visit the bar for a pre-dinner cocktail. Reservations strongly recommended. ⓐ Palais de la Réserve, 60 blvd Franck Pilatte ⓣ 04 97 08 29 98 ⓦ www.jouni.fr ⓛ Daily ⓝ Bus: 20, 30

ENTERTAINMENT

Bar des Oiseaux A Nice institution, this bar/restaurant/theatre began life as a fictional creation in comedienne Noëlle Perna's radio show and she opened the real version in 1998. The live jazz adds to the atmosphere and there's also a 50-seat theatre putting on local productions (often in broad Niçois). ⓐ Corner of rue St-Vincent and rue de l'Abbaye, near place du Palais ⓣ 04 93 80 27 33 ⓦ www.bardesoiseaux.com ⓛ 12.00–14.00, 19.30–23.00

Ghost A small and lively disco and bar whose DJs spin jazz, house and trip-hop. ⓐ 3 rue Barillerie ⓣ 04 93 92 93 37 ⓛ 19.30–02.30

Guest Head to the eastern side of the port to dance with the swish crowds stepping off their yachts. ⓐ 5 quai Deux Emmanuel ⓣ 04 93 56 83 83 ⓦ http://leguest.com ⓛ 23.00–05.00 ⓝ Bus: 1, 2, 7, 9, 10, 14, 81, 100

Opéra de Nice A full programme of concerts, ballet, recitals and opera, October to June. ⓐ 4–6 rue St-François-de-Paule ⓣ 04 92 17 40 00 ⓦ www.opera-nice.org

Pubs If a noisy pub atmosphere with music and possibly karaoke are what you're after, your best options are **Thor** ⓐ 32 cours Saleya and **Ma Nolans** ⓐ 2 rue St-François-de-Paule.

Wayne's This well-established bar/restaurant/club and self-styled 'crazy cultural melting pot' offers a disco, live bands and theme nights. ⓐ 15 rue de la Préfecture ⓣ 04 93 13 46 99 ⓦ www.waynes.fr ⓛ 12.00–01.30 .

VIEWS & WALKS

Take an evening stroll from the newly pedestrianised place Garibaldi, down the rue Cassini to the port. The port itself is magical at night, and one of the music bars around the harbour is likely to tempt you in for a drink or two. Continue along the quai Lunel and around the headland of the Château hill.

War memorials are not usually much of a tourist sight, but Nice's colossal Monument du Morts (dedicated to the 4,000 Niçois who died during World War I) is a spectacular illuminated monument looking out to sea from the hillside. The views out to the Mediterranean from here are unforgettable, and as you round the quai Rauba Capéu you see the entire Baie des Anges magically defined by the lights of the seafront.

From mid-July to September the city stages a 'promenade-spectacle', La Castellada (see below). Actors and musicians accompany an audience on a walk of the Château hill, stopping from time to time to portray the history of Nice, from the Ancient Greeks to the present day, through drama, comedy and music. You don't need a command of French to enjoy the spectacle.

La Castellada ⓐ Walks start from the lift to the Château (see pages 64–6); Concerts in the old Château cathedral ⓣ 04 93 84 86 11 ⓛ 20.30 for a 21.00 start, Tues–Sat, mid July–end Aug. Admission charge; bookable through the tourist office

Western Nice

Most of the sights and activities of this district are confined to the busy area extending a half-dozen blocks west of av. Jean Médecin and south of blvd Victor Hugo down to the seafront. Wherever you wander in this section of Nice, don't forget to look up from time to time to enjoy the upper-storey architecture of the streets – all the wealth, frivolity and self-confidence of Nice's heyday is preserved in the wonderful façades of the villas and apartment blocks built in the late 19th century, culminating in the belle époque years before World War I. This is the area that rivals the Old Town in terms of the number of tourists – and the establishments that cater for them. At night, especially, the seafront acts as a magnet for locals and visitors alike, providing hours of free entertainment where the actors are also the audience. Further east and north are one or two isolated attractions that are worth a journey out from the centre, including the unmissable Russian cathedral and several world-class museums.

SIGHTS & ATTRACTIONS

Cathédrale Orthodoxe Russe St-Nicolas (Russian Cathedral)

Well north of the centre of town, this has become Nice's most-visited single attraction, and remains the largest Russian Orthodox church outside the motherland. In a villa on this site in 1865 Grand Duke Nicholas, son and heir to the Russian Imperial throne, died at the age of 21. The aristocratic Russian expatriate community, led by the Czar and Czarina, had this basilica erected in his memory. It was completed in 1912, just before the Bolshevik Revolution swept away the society that built it, but was further enriched by ecclesiastical

🔵 *The fairytale Russian cathedral*

treasures that the fleeing nobility smuggled out of Russia. Today it is the mother church of Nice's new Russian community and its gilded onion domes guard a jewel box of icons and opulent frescoes. The self-guide sheets given to visitors explain the iconography in great detail and there is a nice selection of reproduction icons for sale in the vestibule. As you walk along blvd Tzarewitch to the cathedral from the bus stop, glance to your right to admire the art deco façade of the apartment block known as Le Palladium. ⓐ blvd du Tzarewitch, north of the main railway station ⓣ 04 93 96 88 02 ⓦ www.egliseorthodoxerusse-nice.com ⓛ 09.00–12.00, 14.30–18.00, May–Sept; 09.15–12.00, 14.30–17.30, Oct & mid-Feb–Apr; 09.30–12.00, 14.30–17.00, Nov–mid-Feb ⓥ Bus: 4, 7 to Thiers-Gambetta; then walk under the motorway bridge to cross the road and turn left into blvd Tzarewitch. Admission charge

Promenade des Anglais

The parasol-bedecked beaches, grand hotels and casinos of the promenade des Anglais, which takes its name from the wealthy British residents who built it for their seaside strolls in the early 19th century, typify the glamorous side of Nice. Today visitors from every country in the world stroll, rollerblade or jog along the world's most famous seaside prom, accompanied, it has to be said, by a ceaseless flow of traffic, while the wealthy patrons of hotels such as the Negresco and West End breakfast, lunch or sip cocktails on their glass-shielded terraces. The promenade connects with the central place Masséna via the avenue de Verdun, which along with the nearby rue de Paradis and avenue Gustave V is the favoured retail location of such upmarket icons as Cartier and Chanel. Between Verdun and avenue des Phocéens lies the park of the **Jardin Albert 1er**, which contains a jolly carousel for kids of all ages and the open-air **Théâtre de Verdure**, scene of the free Musicalia concerts and other events.

Marking the inner part of the promenade (which carries on west for several kilometres as far as the airport) stands the pink and white wedding cake of the **Hôtel Negresco**, the *grande dame* of Nice hotels since 1912 (see pages 38–40). Like many old ladies, she is both stately and a little frivolous – how many hotels of her class would feature a multi-coloured plastic jazz musician (albeit created by French contemporary artist Niki de Saint-Phalle) outside their front door?

The imposing building opposite the Negresco is the **Villa Masséna**, the former home of a descendant of Marshal Masséna (see page 15). This houses the **Musée Masséna**, a collection centred around the history of Nice and the early 19th century, including Napoleon's coronation robes. Unfortunately, the museum has been closed for restoration for some years, though it may reopen in 2008.

Further east along the promenade is the art deco façade of the **Palais de la Méditerranée**. What the Negresco was to the belle époque, the Palais became for the Jazz Age – the hotel of choice for millionaires, presidents and the stars. Built by the Dalmas brothers for American millionaire Frank Gould in 1930, it was the wonder of the age, with a 1,000-seater theatre and a casino. By 1978 it was derelict; the state declared the façade a national building, but the remainder was demolished. Now a new grand hotel and casino sit, rather uncomfortably, behind Gould's masterpiece. Two blocks along, Nice's other casino, the **Casino Ruhl**, occupies the ground floor of the Meridien hotel. Ⓝ Bus: 11, 52, 59, 60, 62, 94, 98, 200, 400, 500, 710, 720

Rue de France & Rue Masséna

The side-streets leading up from the promenade are a mix of designer stores, nightclubs, grocery stores and fast-food outlets. Running along the top of them is the rue de France, which is pedestrianised from the junction with rue du Congrès. Nearby, facing the little place Christine Mane, is one of the few historical monuments in this part of Nice, the **Croix de Marbre**, a marble cross erected

The art deco façade hides a modern hotel

in 1568 to celebrate a meeting between the three most powerful men in Europe at the time: Pope Paul III, the Holy Roman Emperor Charles V and King François I of France. Opposite the Cross, a column commemorates visits by a later pope, Pius VII. In rue de la Buffa, just north of rue de France, is a little piece of England, the **Anglican Church**, built for the British expatriate community in 1862. The surrounding English cemetery dates from 1820. The remainder of rue de France, leading through rue Masséna to the very centre of the city at place Masséna, is a bustling pedestrianised thoroughfare with wall-to-wall restaurants, bars and shops, thronged with visitors and street entertainers. Busy but not too tacky, it has enough to keep the dedicated shopper or diner occupied for days.

CULTURE

Musée d'Art Naïf Anatole Jakovsky (Museum of Naive Art)

The Jakovsky Museum, one of Western Nice's trio of destination museums, opened in 1982 in the Château Sainte-Hélène, the former residence of the parfumier François Coty. It contains around 600 paintings, drawings, engravings and sculptures that chart the world of naive art from the 18th century to the present, including works by Bauchant, Bombois, Rimbert and Séraphine, and Croatian, Haitian and Brazilian artists. ❸ Château Ste Hélène, av. de Fabron ❶ 04 93 71 78 33 ❹ 10.00–18.00 Wed–Mon ❻ Bus: 9, 10, 11, 12, 23, 34 to Fabron-Musée d'Art Naïf. Admission charge

Musée des Arts Asiatiques (Oriental Art Museum) & Parc Phoenix

This 1998 minimalist building, designed by Japanese architect Kenzo Tange to embody Asian philosophical principles, is a work of art in its own right. The museum comprises a series of individual galleries, each devoted to a different Eastern civilisation, from China and Japan to Cambodia and India. There is also a Japanese tea room, where you can experience an authentic tea ceremony, and a multimedia centre for further study of Asiatic culture. The museum stands in the grounds of Parc Phoenix, which has 7 hectares (17 acres) of floral displays laid out on an ecological theme, plus the world's largest glasshouse, featuring tropical plants. The park puts on a varied programme of exhibitions; for details visit ❿ www.nice.fr and follow links under 'Nice Métropole'. Although these two attractions are a bus journey to the edge of town, they're well worth the trip. ❸ 405 prom. des Anglais, near the airport ❶ 04 92 29 37 00 ❿ www.arts-asiatiques.com ❹ 10.00–18.00, Wed–Mon May–mid-Oct; 10.00–17.00, mid-Oct–Apr ❻ Bus: 9, 10, 23 to Arénas. Admission charge

Musée des Beaux-Arts J Chéret (Fine Arts Museum)

This museum stands in the western suburb of Les Baumettes. The beautiful former private villa of a Russian princess, built in 1876, houses a fine collection of paintings, from 17th-century Italian works to 19th- and 20th-century Romantics and Impressionists, including Degas, Boudin, Dufy and Sisley, as well as sculptures by Rodin and others. It is particularly strong in pieces by Nice's native masters Carle Van Loo and Jules Chéret. ⓐ 33 av. des Baumettes ⓣ 04 92 15 28 28 ⓦ www.musee-beaux-arts-nice.org ⓛ 10.00–18.00 Tues–Sun ⓝ Bus: 3, 8, 9, 10, 12, 22, 23 to Rosa Bonheur or Grosso, or 38 to Musée Chéret. Admission charge. Free to under-18s and free to all on 1st & 3rd Sun of month

RETAIL THERAPY

Fashion boutiques and shoe shops crowd the sides of the *zone piétonne*. None of them stand out as destination shops, but they all offer more individual and original items than the big stores.

Near the eastern end of rue Masséna, leading down from the small place Magenta, is rue Paradis, one of Nice's centres for international designer names, including Max Mara, Armani, Chanel and Sonia Rykiel. Pick up whimsical necklaces and funky jewellery by Niçois designers at **Les Néréides** ⓐ 12 rue Paradis. More famous brand names – Cartier, Hermès, Lacoste, Louis Vuitton, Yves St-Laurent, to name but a few – can be found around the corner on the av. de Verdun and av. de Suede.

TAKING A BREAK

Cafés, bars, pizzerias and ice cream parlours abound in the *zone piétonne* and surrounding streets. Unless otherwise indicated, most open early morning and only shut when the last customer has gone home.

Caffè de la Promenade £ ❶ This neon-lit Italian-style café and ice cream parlour is great for watching the endless procession of life along the seafront. Ⓐ Corner of prom. des Anglais and rue Halévy Ⓣ 04 93 82 54 55 Ⓝ Bus: 11, 52, 59, 60, 62, 94, 98, 200, 400, 500, 710, 720

Karr ££ ❷ Stop here for a light lunch (the daily menu is always a bargain) or a glass of wine. The people-watching at a pavement table is unbeatable. Ⓐ 10 rue Alphonse Karr Ⓣ 04 93 81 18 31 Ⓝ Bus: 3, 7, 8, 9, 10, 14, 22, 52, 59, 94, 200, 400, 500, 710, 720, 750

Love ££ ❸ Sip an outstanding cocktail while seated at one of Love's wide teak tables. A popular spot for local trendies. Ⓐ 13 rue Massenet Ⓣ 04 93 82 17 84

🔻 *Small boutiques cluster in the rue Masséna*

Pingala Bar ££ ❹ Grab a coffee or a cocktail at this Indian-inspired open-air bar, on the hotel's third floor. Best enjoyed at sunset. ⓐ Palais de la Méditerranée, 15 prom. des Anglais ❶ 04 92 14 77 00 Ⓝ Bus: 11, 52, 59, 60, 62, 94, 98, 200, 400, 500, 710, 720, 790

Le Québec ££ ❺ For a more substantial midday pit-stop, a lot of experts rate the pizzas at this busy restaurant as the best in town, and the size of the place guarantees you won't have to wait long, if at all, for a table. Great atmosphere at night, too. ⓐ 43 rue Masséna ❶ 04 93 87 84 21 ❶ 11.00–01.00 Ⓝ Bus: 3, 7, 8, 9, 10, 14, 22, 52, 59, 94 200, 400, 500, 710, 720, 790

La Rotonde £££ ❻ If you're smartly dressed and want to treat yourself, why not book a lunch table at the brasserie in the Negresco – it's nowhere near as expensive as the upmarket ambience might suggest, and you might spot some famous faces. (See details on page 89.)

AFTER DARK

RESTAURANTS

Every national cuisine imaginable is available around this area. If you head off the main thoroughfares into the quieter north–south cross streets you're bound to make your own discoveries and save a little off the bill.

Texas City £ ❼ 'French-Texan' owner Frank Charat lays on a satisfying array of Tex-Mex food and hamburgers, with the bonus of proper cocktails. ⓐ 10 rue Dalpozzo ❶ 04 93 16 25 75 ❶ 12.00–14.00, 19.00–23.00 Mon-Sat, 19.00–23.00 Sun

Noori's £–££ **❽** Well-reviewed Indian restaurant just off the main pedestrianised zone. Mumbai cuisine, good service. **ⓐ** 1 pl. Grimaldi **ⓘ** 04 93 88 80 87 **🕐** 19.00–23.30 **Ⓝ** Bus: 3, 7, 8, 9, 10, 14, 22, 52, 59, 94

Boccaccio ££ **❾** The unmissable blue art nouveau façade signals the place to go for serious seafood, served by serious bow-tied waiters. The paella is the best in Nice. Arrive early or book ahead if you want to sit outside; inside the décor is on a sailing ship theme. **ⓐ** 7 rue Masséna **ⓘ** 04 93 87 71 76 **🕐** 09.30–15.00, 18.00–24.00

◗ *Boccaccio is a Nice institution*

Maison de Marie ££ ❿ This courtyard restaurant, an oasis of calm, is accessed from the busy rue Masséna just by Boccaccio (see left) but is a world away from the bustle of the pedestrian zone. Good Provençal cooking and friendly, attentive service. Booking advisable. ⓐ 5 rue Masséna ❶ 04 93 82 15 93 ⓦ www.lamaisondemarie.com ⓛ 12.00–14.00, 19.00–23.00

Restaurant Keisuke Matsushima (formerly Kei's Passion) **££** ⓫ Try Japanese chef Keisuke's innovative blend of French cuisine with Asian undertones. ⓐ 22 rue de France ❶ 04 93 82 26 06 ⓦ www.keispassion.com

Restaurant Stéphane Viano ££ ⓬ Former chef at the reputable Don Camillo, Stéphane opened his own locale in 2007, focusing on modern Niçois dishes and plates of artsy pasta. Spacious and chic, this spot is definitely to be saved for a special night out. ⓐ 26 blvd Victor Hugo ❶ 04 93 82 48 63 ⓝ Bus: 3, 7, 8, 9, 10, 14, 22, 52, 59, 94, 200, 400, 500, 710, 720, 750

La Rotonde ££–£££ ⓭ The convivial atmosphere of Bruno Turbot's brasserie in the Hôtel Negresco includes an indoor fairground carousel, and the set menu is very reasonably priced. Booking advised. For more formal and expensive dining in opulent Regency surroundings, book for the Michelin-starred restaurant **Le Chantecler** – same location, same chef. ⓐ Hôtel Negresco, 37 prom. des Anglais ❶ 04 93 16 64 00 ⓦ www.hotel-negresco-nice.com ⓛ 07.00–23.30 ⓝ Bus: 11, 52, 59, 60, 62, 94, 98, 200, 400, 500, 710, 720, 790

ENTERTAINMENT

The area just behind the promenade is the place to hunt out late-
night clubs and bars with dancing; some also feature cabaret with
showgirls. These streets can get a bit sleazy late at night, so don't
leave a disco alone. Smart dress and a small entrance fee (and your
passport, if you intend to gamble) will get you into the two big
casinos on the promenade. A casino visit can be a complete night
out – both have bars and restaurants that are a big attraction in
themselves, and both put on special themed nights (Creole, Spanish,
Tex-Mex evenings, and so on) in the summer season. For a separate
admission charge you can watch a Vegas-style show and dance to
a disco afterwards at the Ruhl, and the Palais stages cabaret and
other performance events during the winter, and also hosts the
Miss Nice contest.

Le Before Keep your eyes peeled for Le Before's unassuming doorway
– this is one of the best places to enjoy cool cocktails and great DJs
until the early hours of the morning. In warm months, get there

KNOW YOUR ROULETTE
For the uninitiated, French roulette is the kind where everybody
crowds round the table, while the English version has a limited
number of table seats, and the players all bet in chips of their
own colour (so much more orderly). American roulette gives
the bank two chances of taking everyone's money, with a zero
and a double zero on the wheel.

before 22.00 to enjoy happy hour (complete with snacks) on the terrace. **②** 18 rue Congrès **☎** 04 93 87 85 59 **🕐** 18.00–00.30 Mon–Sat, closed Sun **Ⓝ** Bus: 217

Casino Ruhl has 350 slot machines and 5 blackjack, 6 English and 5 French roulette and 4 poker tables. **②** 1 prom. des Anglais **☎** 04 93 03 12 22 **Ⓦ** www.lucienbarriere.com **🕐** 10.00–dawn **Ⓝ** Bus: 11, 52, 59, 60, 62, 94, 98, 200, 400, 500, 710, 720, 790

Palais de la Méditerranée has 4 blackjack, 2 stud poker, 6 American and 2 French roulette tables. **②** 15 prom. des Anglais **☎** 04 92 14 68 00 **Ⓦ** www.lepalaisdelamediterranee.com **Ⓝ** Bus: 11, 52, 59, 60, 62, 94, 98, 200, 400, 500, 710, 720, 790

HITTING THE PROMENADE

Everyone in Nice hits the promenade des Anglais at night at least once a week. The local youth take to their cars and motorbikes, while everybody else walks up and down. This is Nice's version of the Italian *passeggiata*, and the point is just to see and be seen and to take in the night-time views of the light-fringed bay. In the summer you may well be able to catch a free concert at the Théâtre de Verdure, but if not there will be plenty of home-grown talent – musicians and performers – on the seafront. The beach is as popular as during the day for impromptu picnics, volleyball games or just hanging out (but leave when the crowds start to thin out – it's not the safest place at night – and *never* be tempted to sleep out on it).

Eastern Nice

East of avenue Jean Médecin, Nice is a collection of disparate areas and suburbs, without any specific focus except for the 'green belt' of the Paillon (Nice's river, now covered in parks and squares). Walking eastwards from here leads to the area just north of the port, which includes place Garibaldi and the Terra Amata Museum. Further east of the centre are the hillsides of Mont Alban and Mont Boron, which are good for a quick escape into the fresh air. Last but not least, the northern middle-class suburb of Cimiez has a clutch of cultural attractions that easily justify the bus journey.

SIGHTS & ATTRACTIONS

Cimiez

The quiet suburb of Cimiez, standing on what was the Roman settlement of Cemenelum, is home to a whole clutch of attractions, all next to one another. Tucked away in a quiet side-street at the southern tip of the suburb is one of Nice's must-see sights, the **Musée national Message Biblique Marc Chagall**. Further north lie the other major cultural draws, the Arènes, Museé Matisse and the Franciscan Monastery, all close together and served by the same bus stop. As you approach by bus you can't miss an enormous building with monogrammed windows; now an apartment block, this was once the hotel Excelsior Regina, where Queen Victoria stayed on her visits to Nice. It was also Matisse's home throughout much of the 1940s and '50s. The **Musée Matisse** stands across the street in the grounds of the **Arènes de Cimiez**, the remains of the original 4,000-seater Roman amphitheatre (a small one by Roman standards). Today the arena still provides entertainment for the citizens, most

Eastern Nice

Parc de Valrose

RUE J CADEI
AVENUE SAINT LAMBERT
AVENUE DE VALROSE
RUE RAIBERTI
AVENUE MALAUSSENA

AVENUE GEORGE V

CIMIEZ

Arènes de Cimiez,
Excelsior Regina &
Musée Archéologique

Jardins de
Cimiez
Musée Matisse,
Monastère Notre-
Dame-de-Cimiez,
Notre-Dame
de l'Assomption &
Musée Franciscain

RUE EDITH CAVELL
AVENUE DE CIMIEZ
AVE COLONEL EVANS
AVE DES ARÈNES DE CIMIEZ
AVENUE GAL ESTIENNE
CORNICHE
ST ROSALIE

le Paillon
BOULEVARD PASTEUR
AVE MARÉCHAL LYAUTEY
VERANY

RUE INFERIEUR
RUE DE L'EAU FRANCHE
RUE DE LA GENDARMERIE
BOULEVARD JEAN BAPTISTE
ROUTE DE TURIN

Musée national
Message Biblique
Marc Chagall

Conservatoire
de Musique

BLVD VILLEBOIS MAREUIL
AVENUE DES ARÈNES DE CIMIEZ
AVE RATTI
AVENUE DE FLIRINEL
AVE DE PROVENCE

CARABACEL

AVE DE L'ARBRE
RUE XV
COURS PÈRE LATASTE
RJ ALLÈGRE

Palais des Expositions

BOULEVARD JEAN
RUE LÉOPARDI
ROUTE DE TURIN

AUTOROUTE URBAINE SUD

BOULEVARD RAIMBALDI
RUE LEPANTE
RUE PERTINAX
RUE LAMARTINE
RUE DES MBROS
RUE VALPERCA FOCH
AVENUE NOTRE DAME
AVENUE MARÉCHAL
AVE DE LEPANTE

TUNNEL ET

AVE ÉMILE BIECKERT

AVE DE PICARDIE

AVE ÉMILE
BIECKERT

BOULEVARD CARABACEL
AVENUE DES
AVE GALLIENI
ESPLANADE KENNEDY
RÉPUBLIQUE
BLVD GAL LOUIS DELFINO
RUE BARBERIS

Palais des Sports
J Bouin
VOIE MALRAUX
RZEL-NOUZAH

Cinémathèque
Acropolis

i

**CAMP
LONG**

Nice Étoile

AVENUE
GEORGES CLEMENCEAU
RUE PAGANINI
AVENUE
MÉDECIN
BOULEVARD VICTOR HUGO
RUE BISCARRA
RUE DU DOUCHANE
RUE BLACAS
RUE PASTORELLI
RUE GIOFFREDO
RUE DE LA LIBERTÉ
RUE MASSÉNA

2

3 **4**

Galeries
Lafayette

Espace
Masséna

6

Casino
Ruhl

Jardin
Albert ler

i

AVENUE DE VERDUN
PL DES PHOCÉENS
RUE DE FRANCE

QUAI DES ETATS-UNIS

Baie des Anges

BOULEVARD DOUMER
RUE PASTORELLI
HÔTEL DE L'HOTEL
RUE GIOFFREDO
RUE PASTORELLI

Lycée
d'État
Masséna

RUE DEFLY
AVE DESAMBROIS
BOULEVARD CARABACEL

AVE GALLIENI

MAMAC **1**

Théâtre de
Verdure
5

**QUARTIER DES
ANTIQUAIRES**

RUE BARLA

Castel des
Deux Rois

RUE SCALIERO
RUE CASSINI
RUE BONAPARTE

Notre-Dame
du Port

AVE FÉLIX FAURE
BOULEVARD JEAN JAURÈS
RUE DE LA PRÉFECTURE
RUE BOSIO
RUE ST FRANÇOIS-DE-PAULE
COURS SALEYA

Jardins
Suspendus

RUE DE LA LOGE
RUE ROSSETTI

Cemetery

RUE CATHERINE SÉGURANE

PL
GARIBALDI

QUAI CASSINI
Mont Alban,
Terra Amata
Bassin
Lympia

QUAI CASSINI
QUAI LUNEL

VIEILLE VILLE

Colline du
Château

QUAI RAUBA CAPÉU

Palais de
Justice

Bassin
des
Amiraux

Mont Boron

Bassin du
Commerce

QUAI DE DOCKS
BOULEVARD DE STALINGRAD
BLVD FRANCK
PILATTE

RUE DE FORESTA
QUAI DE LUNEL

Corsica

	POI
†	Cathedral
i	Information
✚	Police Station
✈	Airport
🚆	Railway Stn
🚌	Bus Station
✚	Hospital

Eastern Nice

0 ____ 300 metres
0 ____ 300 yards

🔺 *The remains of Roman Nice at the Arènes de Cimiez*

notably at the Jazz Festival. Nearby, the **Musée Archéologique** puts
the visible remains of the Roman town in context. A short walk
away is the **Monastère Notre-Dame-de-Cimiez** (the old Franciscan
Monastery) and its associated church of **Notre-Dame de l'Assomption**.
The monastery garden is a peaceful oasis of rose beds, next to
a cemetery in which the artists Matisse and Dufy are buried. The
monastery cloisters host open-air concerts in summer, and the
Franciscan Museum is worth a visit. 🔵 Bus: 15, 17

Mont Boron

In theory, if you keep walking eastwards you'll reach the commanding
hill of Mont Boron, Nice's biggest open space and a great place to
unwind from the bustle of the city. In practice, it's easier to take a bus
from the city centre: if you catch no. 82 from the bus station you should
get off at the Route Forestière stop on the northern slopes, from where
you can walk to the massive 16th-century fortress of Mont Alban,

222 metres (728 ft) above sea level, affording exceptional panoramic views of the Riviera and Italy. Alternatively, take bus no. 14 from place Masséna all the way to its terminus on the summit of the Parc Forestier du Mont Boron. By walking down the footpaths towards the sea from here you will eventually find yourself back on a bus route, the no. 81, which will deposit you back at the *gare routière*. With its 142 pine-clad acres, 11 km (7 miles) of marked pathways and rare species of wild flowers, the forest of Mont Boron is a favourite haunt of joggers, botanists and walkers. There are magnificent views of St-Jean-Cap-Ferrat to the east and the Baie des Anges to the west.

North & East of the Port

Across the blvd St-Sébastien from MAMAC lies the pedestrianised place Garibaldi, an elegant 18th-century square, which was where Nice first expanded from the medieval confines of the Vieille Ville. The statue of Garibaldi, hero of Italian reunification, who was born in the city, looks on. Continuing along the rue Cassini, past the Quartier des Antiquaires (see page 72), and ignoring the many signs for the Foreign Legion recruitment office, you arrive at the neoclassical church of Notre-Dame du Port, whose statue of the Virgin overlooks the bustle of the Bassin Lympia. Beyond the port is the little hill of Castel des Deux Rois, with its children's amusement park and the prehistoric site of Terra Amata (see page 101).

Le Paillon

Place Masséna was pedestrianised in 2007 in preparation for the long-awaited tram system, and is now home to a gorgeous gigantic fountain, located at the southern edge of the place. Leading east out of the place Masséna is avenue Félix Faure, the northern flank of the continuous open space marking the old course of the river Paillon.

Espace Masséna is a large public square with fountains and greenery, looking across to the towers of the Old Town, which hosts local events and parades from time to time. Over the *gare routière*, the central bus station, is the rather grandly named terrace of the **Jardins Suspendus** or Hanging Gardens of the Paillon, which face the immense **Lycée d'Etat Masséna**, built in an exuberant style of decorated towers and cornices, a kind of Mediterranean Seaside Gothic.

Another hard-to-miss building is the vast grey monolith which houses **MAMAC** (see page 98) and the public library; further north still are the **Acropolis** conference centre, with the **Cinémathèque** (see below) at its far end, and the **Palais des Expositions** trade fair hall.

CULTURE

Eastern Nice is rich in cultural attractions; even if you only visit a few of the museums and galleries listed below you will still experience some of the best of the city's masterpieces.

Cinémathèque

Founded in 1976 by Henri Langlois and dedicated to international film heritage, the Cinémathèque presents an ever-changing programme of classic films, on themes based around the work of a director or performer. It also works to preserve classic films and hosts conferences. To view the forthcoming programme, visit the website; to see a film you need only turn up, become a subscriber for a fee of €1, and then pay a modest €2 per film. ❸ At the north end of the Acropolis centre, 3 espl. Kennedy ❶ 04 92 04 06 66 Ⓦ www.cinematheque-nice.com Ⓛ Sept–July Ⓝ Bus: 3, 6 to Acropole

❶ *The elegant Espace Masséna is a gateway to the Vieille Ville*

Musée Archéologique de Nice-Cimiez (Archaeological Museum of Nice)

The museum charts the history of civilisation in Nice and the
Alpes-Maritimes region (of which Nice was the Roman capital).
The collection includes well-preserved Roman baths dating back to
the second and third centuries AD, as well as ceramics, glass, coins,
jewellery, sculptures and tools ranging from the Bronze and Iron
Ages to the Dark Ages. A small shop offers reproductions of some
of the exhibits. ❸ 160 av. des Arènes ❶ 04 93 81 59 57 ❹ 10.00–18.00
Wed–Mon, closed Tues & some public holidays ❷ Bus: 15, 17 to Arènes.
Admission charge; free on 1st & 3rd Sun of month

**Musée d'Art Moderne et d'Art Contemporain – MAMAC
(Modern Art Museum)**

The permanent collection, dating from 1990, is dedicated to the
related schools of French Nouveau Réaliste and American pop art,
and pays particular attention to the Nice School of the last 30 years.
There is a constantly changing programme of temporary exhibitions.
Not only a must for all serious students of modern art, the pop art
collection is fun for the casual visitor, too. ❸ prom. des Arts
❶ 04 93 62 42 01 ❿ www.mamac-nice.org ❹ 10.00–18.00 Tues–Sun,
closed Mon & some public holidays ❷ Bus: 3, 5, 6, 16, 17 to prom. des
Arts. Admission charge; free on the 1st & 3rd Sun of month

Musée Franciscain (Franciscan Museum)

Part of the Franciscan Monastery of Cimiez, this museum is devoted to
St Francis of Assisi and the history of the order he founded, through
paintings, sculptures, engravings, illuminated manuscripts, frescoes,
and a reconstructed chapel and monk's cell. ❸ pl. du Monastère
❶ 04 93 81 00 04 ❹ 10.00–18.00 Mon–Sat, closed Sun & public
holidays ❷ Bus: 17 to Monastère

⬥ *MAMAC's uncompromising architecture is hard to miss*

Musée Matisse

Housed in and underneath a handsome red-painted 17th-century villa next to the Arènes de Cimiez, the original collection was donated by the artist himself in 1953. In addition to his paintings, drawings, engravings and sculptures, many of his favourite possessions are on display. Henri Matisse, who along with Dufy is the best-known artist of the Fauve school, lived in Nice from 1917 until his death in 1954. The works on show range from his earliest paintings of 1890 to his famous gouache cut-outs, and the museum holds a copy of every book he illustrated. There is also a well-stocked shop for prints and other souvenirs of Matisse and other French artists. ⓐ 164 av. des Arènes de Cimiez ⓣ 04 93 81 08 08 ⓦ www.musee-matisse-nice.org

🕐 10.00–18.00 Wed–Mon, closed Tues & some public holidays
🚌 Bus: 15, 17 to Arènes. Admission charge; free on 1st & 3rd Sun
of month

**Musée national Message Biblique Marc Chagall
(Chagall Museum of the Message of the Bible)**
This museum is one of the cultural highlights of any stay in Nice.
It was opened in 1972 through the efforts of Chagall himself, to
house his enormous body of work on Biblical themes, consisting
of paintings, sculptures, stained-glass windows, mosaics and
tapestries, preparatory sketches, gouaches, engravings and
lithographs. The 17 large canvases that are the highlight of the
exhibition were painted between 1954 and 1967; Chagall's

MARC CHAGALL
Born 1887 into a poor Orthodox Jewish family in Vitebsk, now
in Belarus, Chagall spent his early career in St Petersburg and
Paris, where he mixed with the Fauvists, Surrealists, Cubists
and other avant-garde artists of the day. After a brief spell as
an official artist in Bolshevik Russia, he wandered between
Berlin, New York and Paris, developing a unique style in which
brilliant colour and the frequent reappearance of a range of
iconic characters are the most obvious elements. In 1949
Chagall settled in the Nice area, as had Matisse and Picasso,
and he died in St-Paul-de-Vence at the age of 97. He mastered
an astonishing range of media, from stained glass to lithography.
A deeply religious man all his life, he was inspired by a visit to
the Holy Land in 1930 to begin his Biblical masterpieces.

interpretations of the *Creation of Man* and *The Garden of Eden* are particularly stunning. There are also temporary exhibits of other themes to which he returned again and again, such as the circus. The building itself is the work of André Hermant, a follower of Le Corbusier, and stands in a small garden. The on-site shop sells books and excellent reproductions of Chagall's works. 🅰 av. du Dr Ménard, corner of blvd de Cimiez 🔕 04 93 53 87 20 🔵 www.musee-chagall.fr 🕐 10.00–18.00 Wed–Mon, closed Tues, July–Sept; 10.00–17.00 Wed–Mon, closed Tues, Oct–June 🔵 Bus: 15 to Musée Chagall. Admission charge

Musée de Paléontologie Humaine de Terra Amata (Museum of Human Prehistory)

Taking its name from the earliest inhabited site to be excavated here, this well-arranged museum is devoted to the seven-million-year history of humans, and specifically the last 900 millennia. The area around Nice is one of the longest-inhabited sites in Europe and rich in the remains of prehistoric man. The story that Terra Amata tells is fascinating anyway, but the local finds add a special relevance; it's not everywhere that possesses a 400,000-year-old camp of elephant-hunting *Homo erectus*, who predated *Homo sapiens* by over 350,000 years and seems to have developed communication skills. Ever-changing temporary exhibitions add to the experience and the museum shop is a good place for unusual souvenirs. 🅰 25 blvd Carnot 🔕 04 93 55 59 93 🔵 www.musee-terra-amata.org 🕐 10.00–18.00 Tues–Sun, closed Mon & some holidays 🔵 Bus: 81 to Gustavin (nearest stop), or Bus: 1, 2, 9, 10 to Port Arson, a walk of about 200 m from the museum. Admission charge; free on 1st & 3rd Sun of month

RETAIL THERAPY

The east side of avenue Jean Médecin is dominated by the Galeries Lafayette department store on the corner of place Masséna, and two blocks north there's a day's worth of shopping at the multi-storey Etoile centre, with over 200 shops and specialist boutiques, including familiar names such as Habitat. The nearby branch of FNAC sells books (including English-language), CDs and electronic and photographic products, and is the place to buy tickets for concerts and other events. The avenue is also a centre for bags and leather goods, with at least ten dedicated shops. Shops on the streets east of Jean Médecin tend to be for local, practical needs, but include some specialists.

ArtDecoRoom If you're a fan of art deco and other styles of the 1920s and '30s, then this place sells beautiful authentic objects of the period – at a price. There's also a branch in the Quartier des Antiquaires (see page 72). ⓐ 5 rue Gioffredo ⓣ 04 93 92 91 69 ⓦ www.artdecoroom.com

Bruno Charvin Arts Everything a budding Renoir or Matisse could desire; you might not be able to get one of their massive easels onto the plane but there are plenty of other smaller artists' items that make good presents from the City of Art. ⓐ 39 rue Gioffredo ⓣ 04 93 92 99 90

Libération Market Join the locals and head north of the main train station to visit this massive bustling daily market. ⓐ blvd Joseph Garnier, Place Général de Gaulle ⓒ 08.00–13.00 Tues–Sat, closed Sun & Mon ⓝ Bus: 1, 2, 18, 22, 23

▶ *If you're an artist rather than an art collector, head for Bruno Charvin*

La Porcelaine Blanche Scoop up Provencal porcelain pitchers, tableware, French-themed fruit paintings and much more. Time your trip correctly – the sales items are a steal. ⓐ 32 rue de l'Hôtel des Postes ⓣ 04 93 62 11 25 ⓝ Bus: 4, 7, 9, 10

Voyageurs du Monde This is a travel agency, but if you head through the open-plan foyer you'll discover the best travel bookstore in Nice. Many books are in English. ⓐ 4 rue du Maréchal Joffre ⓣ 04 97 03 64 65 ⓝ Bus: 3, 7, 8, 9, 10, 14, 22, 52, 59, 94, 200, 400, 500, 710, 720, 750

TAKING A BREAK

The air-conditioned coolness of the Etoile centre has a lot to recommend it for a coffee-break during shopping; there are two cafés in the atrium (bring your laptop and take advantage of the free WiFi hotspots) and more on each shopping floor. For more traditional outdoor cafés and bars, make for short but sweet rue Biscarra, behind Monoprix, or the blvd Jean Jaurès on the south side of the Paillon green space. If you're visiting the Terra Amata museum, the nearest cafés and lunch stops are in the Port area, where you'll be spoilt for choice. There's also a small café in the garden of the Chagall Museum, but nothing around the Arènes area. If you're planning a day out on Mont Boron, take a picnic.

AFTER DARK

RESTAURANTS
Au Petit Gari £–££ ❶ Friendly and very funny staff serve up traditional pan-French food in a bistro atmosphere. If you stop in for lunch, the amazing €11 set menu includes the dish of the day, a glass of wine

and a coffee. ⓐ 2 pl. Garibaldi ⓣ 04 93 26 89 09 ⓛ 12.00–14.30
& 19.00–22.30 Mon–Sat, closed Sun

Baie d'Amalfi ££ ❷ Satisfying and authentic Italian food and wine
in an elegant arcaded dining room decorated with views of the
Neapolitan coast. Close to av. Jean Médecin. ⓐ 9 rue Gustave Deloye
ⓣ 04 93 80 01 21 ⓦ www.baie-amalfi.com ⓛ 12.30–14.30 & 19.00–22.30
Tues–Sat, 12.30–15.00 Sun, closed Mon & July

Brasserie Flo ££ ❸ A stone's throw from pl. Masséna, this brasserie,
part of the same group that owns the legendary Bofinger and Boeuf
sur le Toit in Paris, is a destination in its own right. Taking its cue from
the original use of its building by the Folies-Bergères, Flo is set out as
a theatre; the diners are the audience and the kitchen is actually on
stage. The dishes are imaginative and very reasonably priced; there's
even a special menu for late-night diners. ⓐ 4 rue Sacha Guitry
ⓣ 04 93 13 38 38; ⓦ www.flonice.com ⓛ 12.00–14.30, 19.00–24.00

Caffé Bianco ££ ❹ It's easy to overlook this tiny restaurant, which
is nestled between a myriad shops. But what a mistake that would be!
Enjoy modern French cuisine in the candlelit atmosphere – go early,
as it tends to fill up very quickly. ⓐ 9 rue Chauvain ⓣ 04 93 13 45 12

Grand Café de Turin ££ ❺ Not far from the edge of the Vieille Ville
on a corner of one of Nice's liveliest squares, this seafood specialist
has been famous for its *fruits de mer* for nearly 100 years. The décor
is plain, the service a bit patchy at busy times, but you're unlikely
to taste better shellfish in Nice. ⓐ 5 pl. Garibaldi ⓣ 04 93 62 29 52
ⓦ www.cafedeturin.com ⓛ 08.00–23.00

L'Univers de Christian Plumail ££ ❻ Original and stylish cuisine from master chef Christian Plumail, at very affordable prices, especially if you order from the set menu, which is changed weekly. ➌ 54 blvd Jean Jaurès ❶ 04 93 62 32 22 ❿ www.christian-plumail.com ❺ Lunch Tues–Fri, Dinner Mon–Sat, closed Sun

ENTERTAINMENT

Eastern Nice is not noted for its lively nightlife, but Cimiez hosts some important annual entertainments, including the following.

Nice Jazz Festival First staged in 1948, this international celebration of the French love affair with jazz features simultaneous performances on several stages, alongside stalls selling instruments, CDs, books and local food and drink. Over 500 musicians participate in 120 separate performances. Artists make for clubs, bars and hotels to continue after their official sessions. The atmosphere of this family-friendly event (with its own 'children's village' for 5- to 12-year-olds run by qualified supervisors) makes for a great evening. ➌ Arènes et Jardins de Cimiez ❶ ticket sales 08 92 70 75 07 ❿ www.nicejazzfest.com ❺ 18.00–24.00, Wed–Wed (8 days), late July

Les Nuits Musicales de Nice This festival of chamber music follows on from the Jazz Festival at the end of July and extends into early August. Two weeks of night-time open-air performances in the cloisters of the Franciscan Monastery in Cimiez. ➌ Opéra de Nice and the Clôitre du Monastère de Cimiez ❶ ticket sales 08 92 68 36 22 ❿ www.hexagone.net/music/nuits_musicales.htm ❺ Late July–early Aug

● *St-Paul-de-Vence preserves its medieval atmosphere*

OUT OF TOWN
trips

Seeing the Riviera

One of the great things about Nice is that it's so easy to leave it. Not that you're necessarily going to tire of the city quickly, but it is the best possible centre for visiting other parts of the Riviera, the mountainous backdrop of the Alpes-Maritimes and even Italy. The excursions in the following chapters are only a few of the days out that are possible using Nice's excellent transport connections.

TRIPS BY TRAIN

A cheap and comfortable way to get around, the excellent coastal rail service from the main railway station, Gare Nice-Ville (see page 51), puts you in touch with the rest of the coast, with literally dozens of trains per day. Buy tickets at the machines found at all railway stations on this route; they are easy to use, have instructions in English and give change. The following is a round-up of destinations and journey times.

Heading east: Villefranche-sur-Mer (6 mins); Beaulieu-sur-Mer (10 mins); Monaco (25 mins); Roquebrune (30 mins); Menton (37 mins) and Ventimiglia (52 mins).

Heading west: Cagnes-sur-Mer (17 mins); Antibes (29 mins); Juan-les-Pins (32 mins); Cannes (40 mins) and Grasse (1 hr 9 mins).

Chemins de fer de Provence The trains of this private rail company depart from their own station, a couple of blocks north of Nice-Ville. You'll need to catch a no. 18 bus from the centre of town to reach the station. Their historic Train des Pignes, the 'Pine-Cone Line' (no one knows for sure where the name comes from) follows the route of the river Var up into the mountains and then swings west to Digne-les-Bains, with plenty of stops in between for those who want to see a mountain village or two and do some walking. The full scenic route takes just over three hours, with four daily trains in each direction. Digne-les-Bains is a quaint, medieval spa town; it's still possible to take the naturally hot waters, which are said to be good for rheumatism. On some weekends from May to October, you can take a special trip along a section of the line on an old steam train; check the timetable on the website under Nice > Digne-les-Bains, then 'Train Vapeur'. ❸ 4 bis rue Alfred Binet ❶ 04 97 03 80 80 Ⓦ www.trainprovence.com Ⓝ Bus: 18 to Chemins de Fer de Provence

TRIPS BY BUS

Buses depart from Nice's *gare routière* (the central bus station on blvd Jean Jaurès). Services are run by Ligne d'Azur (Ⓦ www.lignedazur.com), the bus corporation for the Nice metropolitan area, and the regional TAM (Transport Alpes-Maritimes). Timetables for individual routes are easily found on the Ligne d'Azur website, including the routes covered by TAM. The central bus station is divided into *quais* (platforms, or bays), at which the service numbers and timetables are posted.

Buses will take you to all the places served by the trains, and some that the train doesn't reach. Since 2005, as part of a plan to encourage more people to take the bus, all trips anywhere along the Côte d'Azur are now €1.30. Bear in mind that buses tend to be much slower than trains, but the ride is generally more scenic and the vehicles are air-conditioned and comfortable.

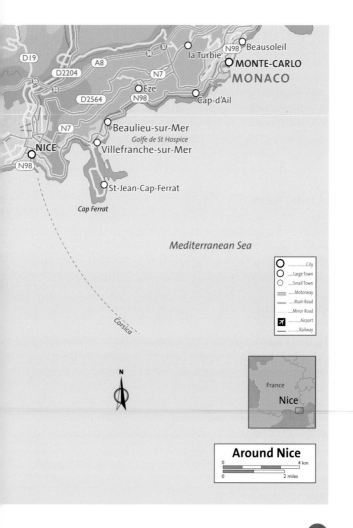

D19
D2204
A8
N7
la Turbie
N98 Beausoleil
MONTE-CARLO
MONACO
Eze
D2564
N98
Cap-d'Ail
N7
Beaulieu-sur-Mer
Golfe de St Hospice
NICE
Villefranche-sur-Mer
N98
St-Jean-Cap-Ferrat
Cap Ferrat

Mediterranean Sea

Corsica

O	............City
O	.....Large Town
O	....Small Town
	....Motorway
	....Main Road
	....Minor Road
✈	....Airport
	....Railway

N

France
Nice

Around Nice
0   4 km
0   2 miles

Villefranche, Cap-Ferrat & Beaulieu

You may not want to do all three of these destinations in one day, but it is perfectly possible. They all lie very close to the city, just east of the promontory of Mont Boron. Villefranche is pretty and historic; St-Jean-Cap-Ferrat is exclusive and upmarket, but also has a zoo and good public beaches; Beaulieu is quieter, catering mainly to an older class of visitor. This excursion also takes in two great attractions, the Villas Kérylos and Ephrussi. If you like sand with your sea, these resorts will satisfy your requirements better than Nice itself.

GETTING THERE

The SNCF train from Nice-Ville station serves Villefranche and Beaulieu; up to 20 departures and returns a day, 6 and 10 minutes' journey respectively. Alternatively, take bus 81 or 100 from Nice central bus station – these offer better views (although no. 100 does not go to Cap-Ferrat).

VILLEFRANCHE

This laid-back and friendly small resort is perfect for families, with a picturesque harbour and a safe, sandy beach. Apart from the beach, there are one or two cultural sights, but it's the small town clinging to the slopes by the harbour that is itself the main attraction. The colourful, pastel-washed houses of this fishing port define a warren of narrow, hilly streets and alleyways, with plenty of cafés and restaurants. One street, the covered alley known as rue Obscure, has been dated back to the 13th century.

Tourist office ⓐ Jardin Binon ⓣ 04 93 01 73 68 ⓦ www.villefranche-sur-mer.com ⓛ 09.00–19.00 July & Aug; 09.00–12.00, 14.00–18.00 Mon–Sat, closed Sun, Sept–June

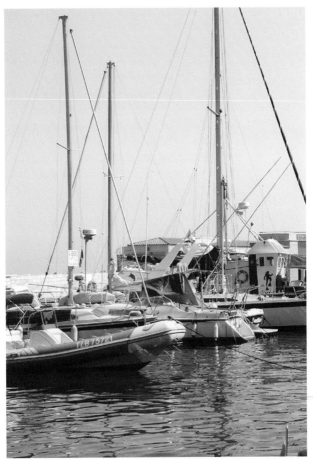

🔺 *No shortage of dive boats at Villefranche*

SIGHTS & ATTRACTIONS

Citadel

The enormous Citadel was built by the Duke of Savoy in 1557 to
defend the port. Villefranche's deep-water outer harbour or rade
has been strategically important for centuries; the Duke's galleys
were stationed here and their commandant resided in the Palais
de Marine on quai Ponchardier. Villefranche remained an important
naval base for the French and latterly the US Sixth Fleet until the
1960s, and used to be a rather raunchier place than it is now. Today
the Citadel houses several historical and art museums, an open-air
theatre and the town hall. There is an entertaining changing of the
guard ceremony outside the Citadel every evening at 19.00 in July
and August, at which two Savoyard pikemen in 16th-century uniform
are relieved by the French army's Chasseurs Alpins, symbolising the
dual military heritage of the fort.

Chapelle de St-Pierre (St Peter's Chapel)

The quayside possesses a star attraction in this 14th-century
fishermen's chapel. The attractive exterior is covered in *trompe-l'oeil*
plasterwork, but it's the interior that draws the visitors, because it
was decorated in 1957 by Jean Cocteau with frescoes depicting the
life and works of St Peter; the result is an artistic tour-de-force.
ⓐ quai Admiral Courbet ⓛ 10.00–12.00, 15.00–19.00 Tues–Sun,
closed Mon, June–Sept; 10.00–12.00, 15.00–17.00 Oct–May.
Admission charge

ACTIVITIES

Beaches

The excellent beach at Villefranche is long and safe for family
swimming and provides all the activity many visitors need, but if

you prefer to get closer to the Med there are plenty of opportunities at Villefranche for boat trips, whale-watching and diving.

Affrètement Maritime Villefranchois This company runs boat trips of 1–2 hours around Cap-Ferrat and as far as Monaco and Menton and back (without stopping); it also offers a 4-hour 'Mediterranean photo safari' to see dolphins and rorqual and cachalot whales. ⓐ Quayside near pl. Wilson ⓣ 04 93 76 65 65 ⓦ www.amv-sirenes.com ⓛ 4-hour safari: 08.30, 13.30 Wed, June–Sept; 09.30 Thur & Fri, July & Aug; 2-hour Monaco trip: 15.00 Wed, June–Sept, 09.30 Wed & 15.00 Fri, July & Aug; 1-hour Cap-Ferrat trip: 17.00 Wed & Fri, July & Aug. Booking essential

Aqua Pro Dive International (Centre de Plongée) Exploration diving, photo diving for children, equipment rental and introductions for beginners. ⓐ 16 rue du Poilu ⓣ 04 93 01 71 04 ⓦ www.apdi-villefranche.com ⓛ Departures 10.00 & 15.00, summer; 10.00 & 14.00, winter

Dark Pelican Hires out a range of motor boats by the afternoon or day. You'll need your passport as proof of identity and will have to leave a hefty deposit in cash or by cheque (not credit card), however. ⓐ Port de la Santé, 1 quai Courbet ⓣ 04 93 01 76 54 ⓦ http://darkpelican.com

RETAIL THERAPY
Brocante market A weekly market devoted to second-hand items of all kinds and qualities. ⓐ pl. Amélie Pollonais & Jardin Binon ⓛ Sun

Provençal market The colourful weekly produce and craft market is a good place to buy Provençal fabrics, local olives and olive oil, clothes and flowers. ⓐ Jardin Binon ⓛ 08.00–13.00 Sat

OUT OF TOWN

TAKING A BREAK

Cafés and ice cream parlours can be found in nearly every street of the Old Town of Villefranche. The comfortable terrace of Beluga in Villefranche (see below) is a particularly good place to sit over a cool drink watching the yachts in the harbour, and if you're serious about boats they keep a rack full of magazines on the subject.

Chez Hiên £ A wide selection of exotic dishes – Indian and Oriental, Greek and Creole – is served up at this restaurant in the Old Town, just one block behind the waterfront. ❷ 4 rue du Poilu ❶ 04 93 01 11 32 🕑 08.00–02.00

Le Cosmo £–££ Across from the Chapelle St-Pierre, this bar and brasserie is equally convenient for lunch after the Saturday market or a late supper or drink. Salads and seafood are excellent, as is their version of anchoïde, an anchovy and tuna dip, served with an enormous basket of raw vegetables. Note that a more limited menu is available between mealtimes ❷ 11 pl. Amélie Pollonais ❶ 04 93 01 84 05 ❿ www.lecosmo.fr 🕑 07.00–02.30

Beluga ££ Delicious tapas and a good range of other dishes are the order of the day at this cool restaurant and lounge bar overlooking the seafront. ❷ 3 quai Ponchardier ❶ 04 93 80 28 34 🕑 12.00–23.00

La Mère Germaine ££ 'Mom' Germaine, 'adopted' by the American Navy officers based in Villefranche, served up traditional French cuisine from 1938 and through much of the 20th century. Today the fantastic restaurant is still family-run. Don't miss the killer wine cellar. ❷ 9 quai Admiral Courbet ❶ 04 93 01 71 39 ❿ www.meregermaine.com 🕑 12.00–13.30 & 19.00–20.30; closed mid-Nov–24 Dec

◼ *Take in the buzz of the quayside at Villefranche*

ACCOMMODATION

Given the short journey time and frequency of the trains, staying in
Villefranche and visiting Nice by day is a viable option, especially if
you're travelling as a family and want to spend plenty of time on the
town's sandy beach. Most options are on or near the main highway,
the Moyenne Corniche, about 10–15 minutes' walk from the
town centre.

Fiancée du Pirate ££ This splendidly named representative of the
reliable Logis de France association has good-value rooms for
families of four. It's quite a way from the town centre, but a good
option if you have your own wheels. ➌ 8 blvd de la Corne d'Or
❶ 04 93 76 67 40 Ⓦ www.fianceedupirate.com

La Flore ££ Another Logis member, in a renovated 19th-century
building, with excellent views onto the harbour of Villefranche.

Good restaurant, too. ❸ 5 blvd Princesse Grace de Monaco
❶ 04 93 76 30 30 Ⓦ www.hotel-la-flore.fr

ST-JEAN-CAP-FERRAT

Cap-Ferrat's green peninsula has been famous for its millionaires' villas since European society started to buy up the real estate in the 19th century, but you won't see much of them beyond their high security gates. If you arrive by bus 81 from Nice you can enjoy a panoramic circuit of the cape, but the more active will find that the 14 km/9 mile coastal path is a walker's paradise. The port of St-Jean, once a fishing village and now a harbour full of upmarket yachts, is a pleasant place for a drink or lunch. There are plenty of minor delights for walkers to discover, including the Chapelle St-Hospice and the lighthouse at the southern tip of the cape.

🔻 *Cap-Ferrat has some of the best beaches on the Riviera*

The **tourist information office** has its own bus stop and is a good starting point, midway between St-Jean and the Zoo. ② 59 av. Denis Séméria ① 04 93 76 08 90 Ⓦ www.ville-saint-jean-cap-ferrat.fr Ⓝ Bus: 81 (which stops at all the sights on the Cap) to Office du Tourisme

SIGHTS & ATTRACTIONS

Villa Ephrussi de Rothschild

More correctly called the Villa Ile de France, this beautiful pink and white confection off the Basse Corniche was built at the beginning of the 20th century. Béatrice Ephrussi de Rothschild was born into a wealthy banking family and spent much of her fortune collecting works of art and antiques to fill the villa she had built. On her death in 1934 the villa was bequeathed to the Institut de France, who now own it. Her real enthusiasm was for the 18th century, which is reflected especially in the priceless porcelain collection. For once, the cliché

▲ *The gardens of Villa Ephrussi are an attraction in their own right*

'treasure trove' is fully justified; you don't have to be an antiques or art enthusiast to be overwhelmed. The gardens are immaculate, too. ❶ 04 93 01 33 09 Ⓦ www.villa-ephrussi.com 🕐 10.00–18.00 1st wk Jan, mid-Feb–June, Sept–mid-Nov; 10.00–19.00 July & Aug; 14.00–18.00 Mon-Fri, 10.00–18.00 Sat & Sun, mid-Jan–mid-Feb Ⓝ Bus: 81 to Plage Passable, Office de Tourisme. Admission charge

The Les Azuriales opera festival, held at the Villa Ephrussi de Rothschild in the first two weeks of August, has been a major event since 1997. Ⓦ www.azuriales-opera.com

Zoo-Parc Cap-Ferrat

This zoo is home to 300 animals and birds, including bears, tigers, monkeys and zebras, and will please younger holidaymakers. 🕐 09.30–19.00, summer; 09.30–17.30, winter Ⓝ Bus: 81. Admission charge

ACTIVITIES

Aside from walking and enjoying the lush scenery, Cap-Ferrat also offers some very nice public beaches. **Passable Plage** is a short walk from the tourist office along the chemin de Passable; **Paloma Plage** is about 1 km/¹/₂ mile south from the port of St-Jean, heading towards the Pointe St-Hospice, and there's another beach just north of the port. Cafés and ice cream parlours can be found near the marina.

BEAULIEU-SUR-MER

The name means 'beautiful place' (according to legend, it was coined by Napoleon when he first laid eyes on it) and the attractions of the site were apparent to the ancient Greek mariners who founded the town. At the end of the 19th century American millionaire and newspaper proprietor Gordon Bennett discovered this tiny fishing village and developed it into a resort for wealthy belle époque visitors, including Edward, Prince of Wales and Gustave Eiffel. Much of the elegant architecture dates from this time, and the town still retains a genteel air. It's the ambience rather than individual sights that attracts visitors, but there are plenty of photogenic buildings, including the Casino and the Chapelle Sancta Maria de Olivo.

Tourist office ⓐ pl. Clémenceau ⓣ 04 93 01 02 21
ⓦ www.ot-beaulieu-sur-mer.fr

SIGHTS & ATTRACTIONS
Villa Kérylos
Just outside Beaulieu stands the 'sister' of the Villa Ephrussi, the Villa Kérylos, also owned by the Institut de France and also the life's work of one obsessive individual. The archaeologist Théodore Reinach was the scion of another wealthy banking family prominent in late 19th-century France. He was inspired to re-create his vision of a patrician Greek palace that stood on the island of Delos in the second century BC, and entrusted the building of his dream villa to an architect who shared his love of archaeology, Emmanuel Pontremoli.

The Villa took six years to construct, following as closely as possible the layout of the remains uncovered on Delos. It was always intended as a house to live in, and the interior, although faithful to the appearance of a classical Greek villa, incorporated all the modern conveniences of the time, cleverly disguised. Today it is a tour de force that delights thousands of visitors. Be sure to pick up a free audiotour to get the most out of your visit. ⓐ Impasse Gustave Eiffel ⓣ 04 93 01 01 44 ⓦ www.villa-kerylos.com ⓒ 10.00–18.00 1st wk Jan, mid-Feb–June, Sept–mid-Nov; 10.00–19.00 July & Aug; 14.00–18.00 Mon-Fri, 10.00–18.00 Sat & Sun, mid-Jan–mid-Feb, mid-Nov–Dec. ⓦ Bus: 81 or 100 to Kérylos. Admission charge

CULTURE & ENTERTAINMENT

Beaulieu hosts a very full programme of concerts and other performances during the summer months – you can get up-to-date details from the tourist office and its website. A regular favourite are the Nuits Guitares in the Jardin de l'Olivaie. If you've caught the roulette bug in Nice, Beaulieu has its own historic and upmarket Casino – check ⓦ www.casinobeaulieu.com for further information.

ACTIVITIES

Beaulieu has two very pleasant beaches, the **Baie des Fourmis** (*fourmis* means 'ants', but don't worry, it refers to the little black rocks that dot the area) and the **Petite Afrique**. Cafés and ice cream parlours can be found near the marina.

RETAIL THERAPY

Beaulieu avoids designer labels and prefers individual small boutiques. As a result, it's well worth checking out for classic rather than youth-oriented fashions.

TAKING A BREAK

African Queen ££ Solid brasserie and pizzeria fare, but a cut above average in terms of quality. A favourite spot with celebrities – the chance of stargazing alone is well worth the visit. ⓐ Port de Plaisance ⓣ 04 93 01 10 85 ⓛ 12.00–23.00

Les Agaves ££–£££ High-end French cuisine, served up in a formal atmosphere in Beaulieu's Palais des Anglais. Try the roasted duck, or their speciality, home-made country pâté. Reservations essential. ⓐ 4 av. Maréchal Foch ⓣ 04 93 01 13 12 ⓦ www.lesagaves.com ⓛ 19.00–22.00; closed 1st 2 wks of Dec

Eze

Eze is well worth a half-day trip from Nice; it is the archetypal *village perché*, an ancient and pretty township sitting 429 m/1407 ft above sea level, with stunning views out to the Mediterranean. More than half a day would be spreading its charms too thinly, unless you plan to use the remainder of your time soaking up the sun in Eze-sur-Mer, the neighbouring seaside village at the foot of the precipice. However, to get from one to the other involves waiting for a bus or a long walk down (only fitness fanatics would do the two places in reverse order). The footpath is clearly signposted and is named after Nietzsche, the German philosopher who used to climb it in the 1880s. It is steep in parts and the steps, where there are any, are quite deep. The advertised time for the descent is 45 minutes, but allow an hour on a hot summer's day.

As at many Mediterranean coastal sites, the population of Eze has moved periodically from coast to hill and back again according to the safety of the times. The Celts inhabited the hilltop village 2,000 years ago. The Romans, living in a more secure age, founded the port of Avisio on the coast; then the Dark Ages brought raids from Moorish pirates, driving the inhabitants to re-fortify the hill – the walls and gates of Eze date from the 14th century. In the 1880s Eze was 'discovered' by Friedrich Nietzsche and from the 1920s to the '50s was the home of Prince William of Sweden, whose villa is now a luxury hotel. In more recent times Eze has seen an influx of celebrity visitors, ranging from President Clinton and Walt Disney (a frequent guest of the Hôtel Chèvre d'Or) to Tina Turner and Naomi Campbell.

GETTING THERE

The best way to see the two sides of Eze in one day is by bus to
Eze Village, then by bus (or on foot down the path) to Eze-sur-Mer,
with a final short ride by train from Eze-sur-Mer back to Nice. From
the *gare routière* in Nice, take either bus 83 or 112 – both leave from
quai 4. There is a bus approximately every 90 minutes on most days,
starting around 07.20; the journey to Eze Village takes about 20 minutes,
depending on traffic. The route takes the Moyenne Corniche –
be sure to sit on the right-hand side of the bus for the best views
on the outward journey. The final approach to the village is over an
impressive early 20th-century viaduct, known locally as the Pont
du Diable ('Devil's Bridge'; according to legend, the bridge-builder
narrowly avoided selling his soul to the Devil).

The SNCF coastal train stops at Eze-sur-Mer, taking a mere
15 minutes, but with no views. Ligne d'Azur bus 83 connects Eze
Village with Eze-sur-Mer: there are just eight buses a day, with long
waits in between – check the timetables to plan your departure as
soon as you arrive at Eze Village – and the service only runs in
May–September. Journey time is about 25 minutes.

Tourist office ❷ pl. du Général de Gaulle, near the bus stop
🕿 04 93 41 26 00 🌐 www.eze-riviera.com 🕘 09.00–19.00, Apr–Oct;
09.00–18.30 Mon–Sat, closed Sun, Nov–Mar

SIGHTS & ATTRACTIONS

It's a short walk up into the Old Town, the original fortified village
once topped by a castle that was destroyed in Louis XIV's time,
through the medieval Postern Gate. The unforced charm of the
narrow pedestrian-only streets, and the views out to sea and across

Until it became fashionable after World War II Eze was still an
agricultural commune and the only feasible means of transport
along its steep narrow lanes was the donkey. Two of the
Provençal breed of donkeys, Nani and Nina, until recently
took luggage up to the Hôtel Château Eza; they can now be
admired in their retirement stable outside the walls.

to the Alpes-Maritimes, are hard to beat. As has often been remarked,
it would be difficult to take a bad photograph in Eze, unless it was
spoilt by other tourists getting in the picture. You have to accept
that many other people have been attracted by the same sights as
you, and the alleys can get a little crowded (so plan to arrive as early
as the buses will let you). Unfortunately for today's tourists, the
14th-century builders of the stronghold planned the narrow streets
deliberately to slow down the advance of invaders.

The oldest building in Eze is the **Chapelle de Saint-Croix** (also known
as the Chapelle des Pénitents Blancs, or Chapel of the White Penitents)
of 1306. The medieval mansions of Eze's wealthier residents have now
become luxury hotels, including the Chèvre d'Or and the Château Eza
(see page 131). The church of **Notre Dame de l'Assomption** was
designed by the Italian architect Antonio Spinelli between 1764 and
1778 to replace an old ruined one. The exterior is relatively plain, but
inside Spinelli let loose with a riot of *trompe-l'oeil*, real windows on
one side being matched by fake ones on the other, a false pulpit
paired with a real one, and so on; this is baroque at its most theatrical.

At the very summit of Eze is the **Jardin Exotique**, begun in 1949 by
the then-mayor on the site of the old castle. Its collection of cacti and

other dry-climate plants is complemented by female statuary by Jean-Philippe Richard, placed in strategic locations to enhance (or detract from, depending on your taste) the stunning views over Cap-Ferrat and the Italian coast. An orientation table lets you work out whether it is really possible to see Corsica, as is claimed. Whether or not you like succulents or statues, the panoramas are worth the entry fee.

Jardin Exotique ⓐ rue du Château ⓣ 04 93 41 10 30 ⓛ 09.00–22.00, July & Aug, 09.00–18.00 or dusk, Sept–June. Admission charge

The seaside part of the town, **Eze-sur-Mer** (also known as Eze Bord-de-Mer), has some good beaches, mostly supervised by lifeguards, and a few cafés and restaurants, as well as the railway station on the main Nice–Ventimiglia line.

RETAIL THERAPY

The old citadel streets are filled with shops selling antiques, craft items and art (both originals and prints). Prices are as you would expect in a place visited by so many tourists, but much of the merchandise is of a better quality than the average tourist trap. In the more modern part of the village there two very popular outlets:

Fragonard The famous fragrance company has a large factory-laboratory just off the main road, at which you can take a multilingual guided tour of the science and craft of perfume-making before visiting the boutique, which stocks a wide range of antique jewellery, embroidered household linen, traditional quilted Provençal *boutis*, glassware and wickerwork, preserves, perfumes, natural aromatic oils and other products. ⓐ Moyenne Corniche ⓣ 04 93 41 05 05 ⓦ www.fragonard.com ⓛ Factory 08.30–18.30 (closed 12.00–14.00, Nov–Jan); Boutique 10.00–19.00 (closed 12.30–14.00, Nov–Feb)

Valery Klein This shop (a branch of a company based in the northern French crystal centre of Baccarat) does a nice line in crystalware gifts, ranging from wine glasses to chess sets to jewellery and objets d'art. ⓐ pl. Général de Gaulle ⓣ 04 93 64 90 65 ⓛ 10.30–19.00 Mon–Sat, closed Sun

TAKING A BREAK

Most cafés and lunch stops congregate in the pl. de Collette, at the foot of the Old Town, near the bus stop. All of them are perfect for a drink or simple meal while you're waiting for your bus to Eze-sur-Mer or back to Nice.

RESTAURANTS

The best restaurants in Eze are those attached to the luxury hotels that cling to the hillside – see under Accommodation. Lunch at one of these need not break the bank, if you're happy to choose from one of the set menus; dinner is always a leisurely gourmet affair and priced accordingly. For the more modest end of the scale, head for the place de la Collette at the base of the citadel.

Le Cactus £ An excellent little restaurant, serving crêpes, sandwiches and salads at a fraction of the cost compared with nearby swish locales. Dine on the terrace to enjoy the amazing views. ⓐ La Placette ⓣ 04 93 41 19 02 ⓛ 11.00–22.00, closed Jan

Cheval Blanc £ Slightly better value than some of its companions. The menu is mainly pizza, standard Italian dishes and salads. ⓐ pl. de la Collette ⓣ 04 93 41 03 17 ⓛ Thur–Tues, closed Wed & Dec

◔ Sample savoury cuisine in Eze's Michelin-starred restaurants

Restaurant le Troubadour ££ In contrast to the haute cuisine of the château hotels and the mass-market offerings of the budget restaurants, this rustic establishment serves authentic and traditional Provençal fare. ⓐ 4 rue du Brec ⓣ 04 93 41 19 03 ⓛ Tues–Sat, closed Sun, Mon & mid-Nov–mid-Dec

Château Eza ££–£££ Michelin-starred cuisine from chef Axel Wagner includes two lunchtime '*Menus saveur*' that are reasonably priced considering their outstanding quality, and a choice of light meals in the afternoon ⓐ rue de la Pise ⓣ 04 93 41 12 24 ⓦ www.chateaueza.com ⓛ 12.00–15.00 (lunch), 15.00–17.30 (tapas and salads only); 19.30–22.00 (dinner), closed Tues & Wed in Jan & Feb

Château de la Chèvre d'Or £££ Opinions vary on whether this or the Château Eza is Eze's leader in the restaurant stakes, but Philippe Labbé's handling of Mediterranean cuisine has many fans. ⓐ Moyenne Corniche, rue du Barri ⓣ 04 92 10 66 66 ⓦ www.chevredor.com ⓛ Closed Nov–mid-Mar

ACCOMMODATION

Eze's popularity with the rich and famous has resulted in some of the most luxurious hotels on the Côte d'Azur. However, cheaper accommodation can be found in the area, including B&Bs and *gîtes*, if you don't mind staying a little way from the Old Town. The tourist office can provide a comprehensive list of all the options. A car is essential if you want to use Eze as a base for extensive sightseeing on the Riviera, though.

Auberge le Soleil £ This villa-style accommodation on the Basse Corniche in Eze-sur-Mer is very close to the sea and has eight comfortable en-suite guest rooms. The good on-site restaurant makes half-board a reasonable option. ⓐ 44 av. Liberté ❶ 04 93 01 51 46 ⓦ www.auberge-lesoleil.com

La Bastide aux Camélias ££ A charming B&B just outside Eze village, with four rooms, a swimming pool, sauna and gardens. Book a wellbeing package and enjoy an aromatherapy massage and use of the hammam and Jacuzzi. ⓐ 3C route de l'Adret ❶ 04 93 41 13 68 ⓦ www.bastideauxcamelias.com ● Closed Dec

Cap Estel £££ For utter extravagance (if you haven't had enough already) and total exclusivity, book a room or suite at Cap Estel, on the shores of Eze-sur-Mer. Former home of a Russian prince, the five-acre estate on a private peninsula has undergone a huge restoration and is now a luxury villa with stunning rooms. ⓐ 1312 av. Raymond Poincaré ❶ 04 93 76 29 29 ⓦ www.capestel.com ● Closed Jan & Feb

Château de la Chèvre d'Or £££ The 24-room Relais & Châteaux hotel, a conversion of several medieval houses in the Old Town, has hosted many celebrity visitors, including Walt Disney, who used to be a frequent guest here. In addition to two swimming pools, stunning views and all the usual top-flight facilities, it boasts three restaurants. ⓐ Moyenne Corniche, rue du Barri ❶ 04 92 10 66 66 ⓦ www.chevredor.com ● Closed Nov–mid-Mar

Château Eza £££ The former home of Prince William of Sweden, this fashionable clifftop hotel has just ten rooms. It perfectly combines an authentic medieval setting with modern facilities and unmatchable views over the sea. ⓐ rue de la Pise ❶ 04 93 41 12 24 ⓦ www.chateaueza.com ● Closed Nov–mid-Dec

St-Paul-de-Vence

St-Paul is another fortified hilltop village beloved of artists, tourists and celebrities. Lying to the west of Nice and some way inland, it doesn't have the sea views of Eze, but the old village inside the medieval walls is larger and the streets a little wider, so even when it gets busy in summer it feels a little less crowded. It also possesses an extra major attraction in the shape of the Fondation Maeght, one of the world's most important collections of modern art, contained in a purpose-built gallery set in an attractive hillside garden.

In the Middle Ages, St-Paul-de-Vence was important enough to be fortified by the kings of France, but by the beginning of the 20th century had become a rural backwater. After World War I it attracted the attention of some of the most illustrious artists of the time, including Picasso, Modigliani, Matisse, Braque and Dufy, all of whom paid for lodging at the (then) humble inn of the Colombe d'Or with their paintings, many of which still hang there. From these beginnings it became a centre of modern art and art dealers and latterly a major tourist destination.

GETTING THERE

Bus 400 departs from quai 5 in Nice's central bus station approximately hourly every day, including public holidays; it can also be boarded on the promenade des Anglais. The journey to St-Paul-de-Vence takes about 45 mins, passing through Cagnes-sur-Mer (about 20 mins from Nice) and continuing on to the town of Vence (about 1 hour from Nice). Bus 94 will take you to Vence and Cagnes-sur-Mer, but it bypasses St-Paul.

▶ *Away from the main shopping streets you can have St-Paul to yourself*

> **DAY TRIPPING**
> Cagnes-sur-Mer, Haute Cagnes (the old medieval town)
> and Vence are all worthy destinations in their own right;
> it is possible to combine a half-day in St-Paul with a visit
> to one of these (to attempt more that two in a day would
> be stretching it). You can also catch a train from Nice-Ville
> station to Cagnes-sur-Mer but not the other destinations.

SIGHTS & ATTRACTIONS

The bus stops outside the tiny medieval Chapelle de Ste-Claire on
the main road. From there it is a short walk past the Colombe d'Or,
now a luxury hotel rather than the humble inn of yesteryear, into
the place de Gaulle. On your right is the large *boules* pitch, which
hosts regional tournaments and celebrity matches from time to
time. At the far end of the place de Gaulle you come to the main
gate of the fortified town, from which leads the principal street, rue
Grande. The tourist office is located on your immediate right. If the
street is already a little crowded, it's better to carry on past the main
gate and make a complete circuit of the ramparts, which hold great
views over the countryside in all directions. At various intervals you
can dive into the town through the narrow connecting streets.

Despite the numbers of visitors, and the obvious commercialisation,
which has turned almost every ancient house into an art gallery or
purveyor of designer chocolates and olive oils, the maze of flower-
bedecked streets retains an irresistible charm. Halfway along, rue
Grande opens out to accommodate the Grande Fontaine of 1850,
for a long time the town's main water supply (always a problem in

the mountains); the water is not drinkable now. The Eglise Collégiale, the church at the top of the Old Town, dates from the 13th century and has an atmospheric interior combining medieval and baroque elements. Facing it across the square is the *Mairie* or town hall, occupying the 12th-century keep of the original castle; next door is the town's museum, the Musée d'Histoire Locale (🕐 10.00–12.00, 14.00–17.00, Dec–Oct; closed Nov). At the far end of the rue Grande and through the porte de Nice, which cuts through the ramparts, lies the town cemetery, which contains the grave of Marc Chagall (see page 100), who died here in 1984.

The small but very helpful tourist office just inside the main gate of the town has good maps and brochures on accommodation and shopping, and offers guided tours; they also rent out sets of *boules* for a game on St-Paul's famous pitch (see left). 🅰 2 rue Grande 🛈 04 93 32 86 95 🔏 www.saint-pauldevence.com

⬇ *At the Fondation Maeght the garden is an art gallery, too*

Fondation Maeght

This world-class art gallery is a stiff 20-minute uphill walk from near the bus stop at Chapelle Ste-Claire. If you have your own car it's not a problem to drive up and use the car park at the gallery; otherwise, older and less agile visitors might find the trek difficult and would be well advised to take a taxi from the stand near the Colombe d'Or.

Aimé Maeght came to the south of France as a Belgian war orphan in 1914 and later opened an art gallery in Cannes. He and his wife Marguerite became friends of most of the leading exponents of art in the inter-war years in France, including Bonnard, Matisse, Braque, Miró, Calder and Giacometti, and through their other gallery in Paris helped to promote their work. In 1964 they set up a private foundation to which they donated their own extensive collection, and the Fondation now owns more than 9,000 works by world-famous modern artists (although they're never all on display at the same time). The striking modern gallery was designed by Catalan architect Josep Luis Sert, and the surrounding garden is decorated with typically quirky figures by Miró and Giacometti. There is no set route through the gallery and no particular plan of arrangement of the ever-changing exhibits, all of which makes the experience one of personal discovery rather than art education. ❸ Montée des Trious, St-Paul-de-Vence ☎ 04 93 32 81 63 🔀 www.maeght.com ⏱ 10.00–19.00, July–Sept; 10.00–12.30, 14.30–18.00, Oct–June. Admission charge

RETAIL THERAPY

If you're seriously contemplating acquiring an original work of art, then you could spend a day in the commercial galleries of St-Paul. Try Galerie du Vieux St-Paul (❸ 16 rue Grande) for a good mix of established and

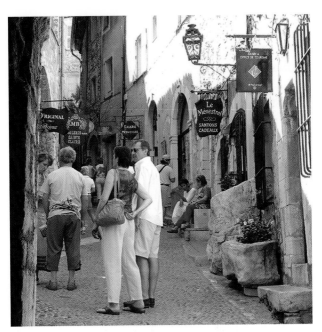

⏶ *There's plenty to tempt the shopper in St-Paul-de-Vence*

lesser-known artists. The town's shops are also strong on furniture, ceramics and other objects of interior design, while other boutiques specialise in figurines, traditional garments and other gifts with a Provençal air. The accent is mostly on authentic, quality goods at a commensurate price, rather than cheap souvenirs, so bring your credit card! The tourist office issues a comprehensive catalogue of local shops to help you find what you're looking for. In addition, there is a small Provençal produce market near the *boules* arena at the entrance to the town on Tuesdays and Thursdays, and on Saturday mornings the same spot overflows with both produce and flowers.

TAKING A BREAK

Fine food at fine prices is not hard to come by in the restaurants of the luxury hotels in and around St-Paul. Luckily, there's also no shortage of simpler establishments good for a morning coffee, cooling drink or simple lunch.

Dolce Italia £ If you've made the climb up the steps to the church you're probably ready for one of the true Italian cappuccinos or ice creams that this café specialises in. ⓐ 13 pl. de l'Eglise ❶ 04 93 24 09 95 ◷ Daily

Malabar £ Calling itself a 'gourmet snack bar', this café on the ramparts serves good-value sandwiches, *pissaladière* and other snacks, and lunches, all to take away or eat on the spot. Everything served is home-made. ⓐ Rempart Ouest ❶ 04 93 32 60 14 ◷ 12.00–15.30 Thur, Sun–Tues, 12.00–15.30, 19.00–22.00 Fri & Sat, closed Wed

Le Tilleul £–££ This busy terrace restaurant is just inside the walls to the left of the town gate. The food is unsophisticated but tasty and service is efficient. In summer it attracts wandering entertainers – children will love it. ⓐ pl. du Tilleul ❶ 04 93 32 80 36 ⓦ www.letilleul-saintpaul.com

Le Saint Paul £££ Mediterranean food doesn't come any better than the Michelin-starred cuisine on the flowery terrace of this Relais & Château hotel. ⓐ 80 rue Grande ❶ 04 93 32 62 25 ⓦ www.lesaintpaul.com ◷ 12.30–13.45, 19.30–21.45, Apr–Oct; 12.30–13.45, 19.30–21.45 Thur–Mon, Mar & Nov–mid-Dec; closed mid-Dec–late Dec & early Jan–Feb

EVENTS

The local tourist authority works hard to make sure its visitors
don't become bored, with a full programme of events ranging
from summer concerts to the folk festival Fête Patronale de
Ste-Claire – three days of traditional costumes, dancing and
processions at the beginning of August. This is followed closely
by four days of *pétanque* competitions that attract devotees
from as far afield as Japan. Autumn sees a heritage weekend in
September and the annual festival of the local wine harvest in
October. The tourist office issues good seasonal lists of all the
organised activities in St-Paul.

ACTIVITIES

St-Paul is a good centre for walking in the surrounding hills,
with marked trails leading from near the Chapelle Ste-Claire on
the main road. If you've never played *pétanque*, you can learn from
a local on the town's famous arena with one of the instruction
packages from the tourist office (see page 135).

ACCOMMODATION

St-Paul has plenty of luxury accommodation to suit its celebrity
visitors. More cost-wise travellers will find lodgings further out of
town, but even if you're not travelling by car it won't matter too
much, as most are close to the main bus route.

Hostellerie les Remparts £–££ One of the few hotels right in the
middle of the Old Town, this traditional stone-built house, with nine

guest rooms and a good regional restaurant, offers a warm welcome.
🄰 72 rue Grande 🛈 04 93 32 09 88

Hôtel le Hameau ££ Within walking distance of the town and
the Fondation Maeght, this charming hotel had Chagall as a guest
many years ago. It has 17 comfortable rooms and a large swimming
pool – and the breakfast marmalade is made with oranges grown
on the premises. 🄰 528 route de la Colle 🛈 04 93 32 80 24
🆆 www.le-hameau.com 🄻 Closed mid-Nov–mid-Feb

Les Vergers de Saint Paul ££–£££ The 15 rooms and 2 suites here are
grouped in a two-storey and a one-storey building around the large
central swimming pool. In a secluded location, but less than 1 km
(½ mile) from the town. 🄰 940 route de la Colle 🛈 04 93 32 94 24
🆆 www.vergersdesaintpaul.com

La Colombe d'Or £££ What was a simple country inn at the time the
artists descended on St-Paul has become a destination hotel and
restaurant that is proud of its celebrity guests and the works of art
that decorate the place (donated in lieu of payment by the likes of
Modigliani and Picasso). The atmosphere is both professional and
relaxed – don't expect the service to be stiff or overly pampering.
You must be a guest of the hotel or restaurant in order to view
their amazing art collection. 🄰 pl. de Gaulle 🛈 04 93 32 80 02
🆆 www.la-colombe-dor.com 🄻 Closed Nov–beginning of
Christmas season

❿ Gare Nice-Ville is the rail hub of the Riviera

Directory

GETTING THERE

By air

Nice-Côte d'Azur airport serves flights from many UK and Irish airlines, including **Aer Lingus** ☎ 08 21 23 02 67 🖥 www.aerlingus.com (from Dublin and Cork), **British Airways** ☎ 08 25 82 54 00 🖥 www.britishairways.com, **British Midland** ☎ 01 41 91 87 04 🖥 www.flybmi.com and **Bmibaby** ☎ 08 90 71 00 81 🖥 www.bmibaby.com (from Birmingham and East Midlands), **EasyJet** ☎ 08 26 10 26 11 🖥 www.easyjet.com (from London Gatwick, Luton and Stansted, Bristol, Liverpool, Newcastle and Belfast) and **Globespan** ☎ 08 70 55 61 522 🖥 www.flyglobespan.com (from Edinburgh and Glasgow). Flight time from London is about 2 hours. Direct flights from other countries include Canada (**Air Transat** ☎ 08 25 12 02 48 🖥 www.airtransat.ca from Montréal) and USA (Air France, **Delta** ☎ 08 11 64 00 05 🖥 www.delta.com from New York JFK).

Many people are aware that air travel emits CO_2, which contributes to climate change. You may be interested in the possibility of lessening the environmental impact of your flight through Climate Care, which offsets your CO_2 by funding environmental projects around the world. Visit 🖥 www.climatecare.org.

By car

If you're coming by car from the UK via Calais, it will take you 2–3 days to cover the 1,200km (745 miles) from Calais to Nice. Head for Marseilles and pick up the A8 *autoroute*, 'La Provençale', to Nice. For the approaches to Nice, see page 52.

By rail

The journey from London St Pancras to Paris Gare du Nord on the
Eurostar and then by TGV from Paris Gare de Lyon to Nice-Ville
averages about 11 hours, and return fares can be cheaper than those
of many low-cost airlines. If you are Inter-railing or Eurailing, you can
reach Nice not only from cities in France but also by direct international
trains. The monthly *Thomas Cook European Rail Timetable* has up-to-
date schedules for European international and national train services.

Eurostar reservations (UK) ⓣ 08705 186 186 ⓦ www.eurostar.com
General rail information ⓦ www.raileurope.com

Thomas Cook European Rail Timetable ⓣ (UK) 01733 416477;
(USA) 1 800 322 3834 ⓦ www.thomascookpublishing.com

ENTRY FORMALITIES
Documentation

Passports are needed by UK visitors and all others except EU citizens
who can produce a national identity card. Visits of up to three months
do not require a visa if your nationality is UK, Republic of Ireland, US,
Canadian, Australian or New Zealand. Other travellers should consult
the French embassy or tourist office in their own country on visa
requirements. ⓦ www.diplomatie.gouv.fr/venir/visas/index.html

Customs

When going to France, residents of the UK, Ireland and other EU
countries may bring personal possessions and goods for personal use,
including a reasonable amount of tobacco and alcohol, provided they
have been bought in the EU. There are few formalities at the point
of entry into France. Residents of non-EU countries, and EU residents

arriving from a non-EU country, may bring in up to 400 cigarettes and 50 cigars or 50 g (2 oz) tobacco; 2 litres (3 bottles) of wine and 1 litre (approx. 2 pints) of spirits or liqueurs. The full regulations and definitions of 'reasonable amount' may be checked at ⓦ www.douane.gouv.fr.

MONEY

The euro (€) is the official currency in France. €1 = 100 cents. It comes in notes of €5, €10, €20, €50, €100, €200 and €500. Coins are in denominations of €1 and €2, and 1, 2, 5, 10, 20 and 50 cents. ATM machines can be found at the airport, railway stations, shopping centres and outside most banks, and they accept most British and international debit and credit cards. They are the quickest and most convenient way to obtain cash, though a charge will be levied. Instructions on use are available in English and other major European languages.

The most widely accepted credit cards are VISA and MasterCard, though other major credit cards such as American Express are also commonly accepted in restaurants and shops. Travellers' cheques have become relatively difficult to cash – seek out a bureau de change, such as the one opposite Galeries Lafayette on av. Jean Médecin. Foreign money can be cashed at most banks and bureaux de change in Nice, though you may have to produce your passport or other ID.

American Express has a bureau de change in Nice. ⓐ 11 prom. des Anglais ❶ 04 93 16 53 53 🕓 09.00–20.00, Oct–Apr; 09.00–21.00, May–Sept; 10.00–18.00 on public holidays

HEALTH, SAFETY & CRIME

Tap water is safe to drink (if not it is marked *eau non potable*) but the French and most visitors prefer to consume one of the many brands of mineral water.

Medical facilities in France are of an excellent standard, but expensive – ensure you have adequate travel insurance. Most minor ailments can be taken to pharmacies, indicated by a green cross sign – the one in the rue Masséna pedestrian zone is 24-hour. Pharmacies have expert staff who are qualified to offer medical advice and dispense a wide range of medicines. Many drugs, such as aspirin, that are widely available in the UK are obtainable only at pharmacies in France.

🔽 *Rue Masséna's pharmacy is always open*

Nice is a safe city, by and large. The beach and the streets west and north of the promenade des Anglais are not the best places to be late at night (and budget travellers should never be tempted to sleep overnight on the beach to save on accommodation costs). Otherwise, take normal sensible precautions – avoid deserted streets by night, keep valuables secure from pickpockets and opportunist bag-snatchers by day. Never leave valuables in a car, as theft from (and of) automobiles is one of Nice's main crime issues. You may encounter one of the hustlers who especially frequent the seafront. A common scam is to 'give' you a worthless ring or trinket and then as the conversation drags on ask for payment of 'whatever you think it is worth'. There are also plausible 'distressed tourists' around – some quite elderly – who will spin you a heartbreaking story of being suddenly penniless and not being able even to phone their consulate. In both cases, simply walking away is normally sufficient to deter the scam operators. Public disorder and drunkenness are rare – so rare that people stand and stare at the occasional drunks (who embarrassingly tend to be foreigners in the Old Town).

OPENING HOURS

Shops 09.00–12.00, 14.00–19.00 Mon–Sat (those on the main pedestrian areas tend to stay open later and don't close for lunch).
Banks 08.30–12.00, 13.30–17.00 Mon–Fri
Note that some museums are closed on Mondays.

TOILETS

Museums generally have good toilet facilities. The average café and restaurant toilet is clean but small and often unisex; the better the establishment the better the facilities. If you want to use the

facilities in cafés, bars and restaurants, you generally have to buy
something first. Public toilets in Nice are the modern, hygienic
coin-operated cubicles (which young children shouldn't be allowed
to use unaccompanied).

CHILDREN

The only health threat to children on the Riviera is the strength of
the sun – ensure that they have adequate protection from it at all
times. If you are travelling with babies or young children you can
buy nappies, baby food and other supplies in supermarkets and
pharmacies. Restaurants are used to children eating with the
family, and junior menus and smaller portions are commonly
offered. Many attractions and transport providers have reduced
rates for children.

There is plenty to keep the kids entertained in Nice and on
the Riviera generally. The most obvious attraction is the beach –
the sandy beaches of **Villefranche** and **Cap-Ferrat**, in particular.
In Nice, the carousel in the **Jardin Albert 1er** facing the seafront
will keep kids amused for a while, as will the 'human statue' street
entertainers in the rue Masséna pedestrian area (though they're
perhaps a bit scary for the very young). It's worth visiting the
Château, too: there's a playground on top of the hill, and a puppet
show on the Château's main esplanade every Sunday afternoon
(16.00–17.00). A ride on the **Petit Train Touristique** (see page 42)
is loved by children and parents alike; the Castel des Deux Rois
mini-amusement park in eastern Nice, between the port and
Terra Amata (see page 101), also has its own *petit train*, along with
mini-golf, giant chessboard, wooden play huts and more. For animal
fun, head to the **Zoo-Parc Cap-Ferrat** (see page 121). There's also
a theme park in the area:

Marineland: Parc de la Mer et de l'Aventure This theme park is just a
short train ride away near Antibes. In addition to the Wild West area,
an aquasplash and adventure golf, the family can enjoy performing
dolphins that can be petted, a pirate ship that lets you get close up
to orcas, a scary shark tunnel and a tropical aquarium. ⓐ Off the N7
highway ❶ 04 93 33 49 49 ⓦ www.marineland.fr ❶ 10.00–22.30,
July–early Sept; closed early Sept–June ⓝ Frequent trains from
Nice-Ville take about 25 mins to Biot station, then it's about 2 mins
on foot from the park.

⬇ *Simple fun for the kids in Jardin Albert 1er*

TELEPHONING NICE

To call Nice from abroad, dial your own international prefix (00 in most countries) then 33 for France. The area code for southeast France, including Nice, is 04, followed by a number which is always eight digits in length. When dialling from abroad, drop the first 0, to leave 00 33 4 and the eight-digit number. When dialling Nice from anywhere in France, dial 04 and then the eight-digit number.

COMMUNICATIONS

Internet

Even some smaller hotels provide an internet connection, but in any case internet cafés are plentiful in Nice. One of the most central is just off the promenade des Anglais:

Nemeos ⓐ 2 rue Halévy ⓣ 04 93 87 37 48 ⓔ contact@nemeos.com
ⓛ 10.00–22.00 Mon–Thur, 10.00–24.00 Fri & Sat, closed Sun

Phone

Card-operated public phone booths are everywhere, and you can make international calls from them. You can buy phonecards (*télécartes*) at *tabacs* (newsagent/tobacconist shops sporting a red diamond sign outside), post offices and some cafés and railway stations.

Post

Post offices can be found all over Nice – the most central ones are in the rue Gassin in the Old Town and on av. Jean Médecin just south of blvd Victor Hugo. They open 09.00–17.30 or 18.00 on weekdays and some close 12.00–14.00. They are also closed on Sat afternoons and all day Sunday. Stamps can be bought there or at *tabacs*. Postcards to the UK and Ireland will normally arrive in 2–3 days, taking a little longer to non-European destinations. Current rates for sending postcards are Europe €0.65, North America €0.90, Australia and New Zealand €0.90.

ELECTRICITY

France runs on 220v with two-pin plugs. British appliances will need a simple adaptor, easily obtained at any electrical or hardware store

● *France has a modern and efficient postal service*

in the centre of Nice. US and other equipment designed for 110v
will need a transformer (*transformateur*).

TRAVELLERS WITH DISABILITIES

The bigger installations, such as the airport and central railway
station, and many of the larger hotels, have access and facilities
adapted for visitors with mobility problems. All road crossings
in Nice are wheelchair-accessible, as is the central section of the
beach, accessed from opposite the Jardin Albert 1er. Elsewhere
the position is less satisfactory, and the steep hills and narrow,
cobbled streets of Eze and St-Paul, for instance, are unsuited to
wheelchair-based tourists. Useful organisations for advice and
information include:

RADAR The principal UK forum and pressure group for people
with disabilities. **a** 12 City Forum, 250 City Road, London EC1V 8AF
t (020) 7250 0212 **w** www.radar.org.uk

SATH (Society for Accessible Travel & Hospitality) Advice for
US-based travellers with disabilities. **a** 347 Fifth Ave, Suite 610,
New York, NY 10016 **t** (212) 447 7284 **f** (212) 725 8253 **w** www.sath.org

**Association des Paralysés de France Délégation Départementale
des Alpes-Maritimes a** 21 blvd Mantéga-Righi, Nice **t** 04 92 15 78 70

TOURIST INFORMATION
Tourist offices
The Nice Convention and Visitors Bureau maintains three offices,
on the seafront and at the airport and the railway station. They
stock a wide range of literature and maps and have helpful staff

who can make accommodation bookings and sell tickets for many attractions and events, including Carnaval.

Office du Tourisme et des Congrès ⓐ 5 prom. des Anglais ⓣ 0892 70 74 07 ⓛ 08.00–20.00 Mon–Sat, 09.00–19.00 Sun, June–Sept; 09.00–18.00 Mon–Sat, Oct–May ⓝ Bus: 11, 52, 59, 60, 62, 94, 98, 200, 400, 500, 710, 720, 790

Office du Tourisme et des Congrès à Nice Côte d'Azur Airport–Terminal 1 ⓣ 0892 70 74 07 ⓛ 08.00–21.00, June–Sept; 08.00–21.00 Mon–Sat, Oct–May

Office du Tourisme et des Congrès ⓐ Gare Nice-Ville, av. Thiers ⓣ 0892 70 74 07 ⓛ 08.00–20.00 Mon–Sat, 09.00–19.00 Sun, June–Sept; 08.00–19.00 Mon–Sat, 10.00–17.00 Sun, Oct–May

Centre Régional Information Jeunesse (CRIJ) Côte d'Azur is an advice and information centre for young independent travellers in eastern central Nice, well-signposted from the middle of town. ⓐ 19 rue Gioffredo ⓣ 04 93 80 93 93 ⓦ www.crijca.fr ⓛ 10.00–18.00 Mon–Fri

Websites

The Nice tourist office website is very informative and includes a comprehensive instant accommodation booking service ⓦ www.nicetourism.com

Additional information and listings, especially of events, can be found on the city council website ⓦ www.nice.fr

Other useful sites include:

Ⓦ www.guideriviera.com (the official site of the whole Riviera)

Ⓦ www.cotedazur-en-fetes.com (events on the Riviera)

Ⓦ http://riviera.angloinfo.com (English-speaking services and information)

If you're trying to track down a business of any sort, use the French Yellow Pages site at Ⓦ www.pagesjaunes.fr, which also provides location maps for all its listings.

BACKGROUND READING

Nice and its environs has long been a hotbed of creative activity for artists and authors alike. To get yourself into the Côte d'Azur mindset, grab F Scott Fitzgerald's *Tender is the Night*, set on the Cap d'Antibes. Ernest Hemingway's *The Garden of Eden* takes place on the French Riviera during the 1920s. James Joyce claimed the idea for *Finnegan's Wake* came to him while visiting Nice, and in 1938, after watching a pianist perform on Cap-Ferrat, Murray Burnett wrote the play *Everybody Comes to Rick's*, on which the film *Casablanca* was based. Jean-Paul Sartre wrote *Les Chemins de la Liberté* in Saint-Tropez, and for a dose of all-American literature, Louisa May Alcott's Laurie and Amy (*Little Women*) fell in love in Nice. For fans of Henri Matisse, pick up a copy of *Chasing Matisse*, James Morgan's chronicle tracing the great artist's career through his places of residence.

Emergencies

EMERGENCY NUMBERS

The following are all national free emergency numbers:

Medical/ambulance (SAMU) ❶ 15

Police/Gendarmerie ❶ 17

Fire (Sapeurs-Pompiers) ❶ 18

Any emergency service ❶ 112 (*Must* be used from mobile phones)

Nice Central Police Station ❶ 04 92 17 22 22 (interpreter) ❶ 04 92 17 20 68

MEDICAL SERVICES

Night pharmacy ❷ 7 rue Masséna ❶ 04 93 87 78 94

Hôpital St–Roch Hospital with 24-hour emergency services.
❷ Entrance on 5 rue Pierre Devoluy ❶ 04 92 03 33 75

Hôpital Lenval Specialising in child health emergencies
❷ 57 av. de la Californie ❶ 04 92 03 03 03

Riviera Medical Services English-speaking doctors on call
(not necessarily for emergencies). ❶ 04 93 26 12 70

SOS Dentaire Emergency dental care at night and on Sundays
& public holidays. ❶ 04 93 76 53 53; 04 92 13 00 99

POLICE

There is a mobile police post in the rue Masséna and regular but low profile patrols in the main tourist areas. The Police Municipale are the most in evidence in Nice itself, overseeing traffic and petty crime; the Police Nationale deal with more serious matters. In country districts and on motorways the Gendarmerie Nationale are the main law enforcement body.

Commissariat Central de Police (Central Police Station) ❸ 1 av. Maréchal Foch ❶ 04 92 17 22 22 🕐 24 hours, interpreters ❶ 04 92 17 20 68

EMERGENCY PHRASES

Help!	**Fire!**	**Stop!**
Au secours!	Au feu!	Stop!
Ossercoor!	*Oh fur!*	*Stop!*

Call an ambulance/a doctor/the police/the fire service!
Appelez une ambulance/un médecin/la police/les pompiers!
*Ahperleh ewn ahngbewlahngss/ang medesang/lah poleess/
leh pompeeyeh!*

Police Municipale (Lost property office) ⓐ rue Raoul Bosio ☎ 04 97 13 44 00
🕒 08.30–17.00 Mon–Thur, 08.30–15.45 Fri, closed Sat & Sun

EMBASSIES & CONSULATES
Australian Embassy ⓐ 4 rue Jean Rey, Paris ☎ 01 40 59 33 00
ⓦ www.france.embassy.gov.au
Canadian Consulate ⓐ 10 rue Lamartine, Nice ☎ 04 93 92 93 22
ⓦ www.international.gc.ca/canada-europa/france
New Zealand Embassy ⓐ 7 rue Léonard da Vinci, Paris ☎ 01 45 01 43 43
ⓦ www.nzembassy.com
Republic of Ireland Consulate ⓐ 152 blvd J-F Kennedy, Cap d'Antibes
☎ 04 93 61 50 63 ⓦ http:// ireland.visahq.com/embassy/france
South African Embassy ⓐ 59 quai d'Orsay, Paris ☎ 01 53 59 23 23
ⓦ www.afriquesud.net
UK Consulate General ⓐ 24 av. du Prado, Marseille ☎ 04 91 15 72 10
ⓦ www.britishembassy.gov.uk
USA Consulate ⓐ 3rd Floor, 7 av. Gustave V, Nice ☎ 04 93 88 89 55
ⓦ www.amb-usa.fr

WHAT'S IN YOUR GUIDEBOOK?

Independent authors Impartial up-to-date information from our travel experts who meticulously source local knowledge.

Experience Thomas Cook's 165 years in the travel industry and guidebook publishing enriches every word with expertise you can trust.

Travel know-how Contributions by thousands of staff around the globe, each one living and breathing travel.

Editors Travel-publishing professionals, pulling everything together to craft a perfect blend of words, pictures, maps and design.

You, the traveller We deliver a practical, no-nonsense approach to information, geared to how you really use it.

SPOTTED YOUR NEXT CITY BREAK?

Then these lightweight CitySpots pocket guides will have you in the know in no time, wherever you're heading. Covering over 80 cities worldwide, they're packed with detail on the most important urban attractions from shopping and sights to non-stop nightlife; knocking spots off chunkier, clunkier versions.

Aarhus	Genoa	Paris
Amsterdam	Glasgow	Prague
Antwerp	Gothenburg	Porto
Athens	Granada	Reykjavik
Bangkok	Hamburg	Riga
Barcelona	Hanover	Rome
Belfast	Helsinki	Rotterdam
Belgrade	Hong Kong	Salzburg
Berlin	Istanbul	Sarajevo
Bilbao	Kiev	Seville
Bologna	Krakow	Singapore
Bordeaux	Kuala Lumpur	Sofia
Bratislava	Leipzig	Stockholm
Bruges	Lille	Strasbourg
Brussels	Lisbon	St Petersburg
Bucharest	Ljubljana	Tallinn
Budapest	London	Tirana
Cairo	Los Angeles	Tokyo
Cape Town	Lyon	Toulouse
Cardiff	Madrid	Turin
Cologne	Marrakech	Valencia
Copenhagen	Marseilles	Venice
Cork	Milan	Verona
Dubai	Monte Carlo	Vienna
Dublin	Moscow	Vilnius
Dubrovnik	Munich	Warsaw
Düsseldorf	Naples	Zagreb
Edinburgh	New York	Zurich
Florence	Nice	
Frankfurt	Oslo	
Gdansk	Palermo	
Geneva	Palma	

Available from all good bookshops, your local Thomas Cook travel store or browse and buy on-line at www.thomascookpublishing.com

Thomas Cook
Publishing

ACKNOWLEDGEMENTS & FEEDBACK

Editorial/project management: Lisa Plumridge
Copy editor: Lesley McCave
Layout/DTP: Pat Hinsley and Alison Rayner
Proofreader: Yvonne Bergman

The publishers would like to thank the following individuals
and organisations for supplying their copyright photographs
for this book: A1 Pix, pages 13, 47, 69, 117 & 118–19; Ivan Cholakov/
BigStockPhoto.com, page 80; Ethel Davies, page 120; William
Howorth, page 23; Office du Tourisme et des Congrès, Nice, page 17;
Kersti Plehhov/BigStockPhoto.com, page 75; Tristan Rutherford, page 129;
Olga Shelego/Stockxpert.com, pages 42–3; Kathryn Tomasetti, pages 5,
19, 21 & 27; Paul Medbourne and Patsy Trimnell, all others.

Send your thoughts to
books@thomascook.com

- Found a great bar, club, shop or must-see sight that we don't feature?
- Like to tip us off about any information that needs a little updating?
- Want to tell us what you love about this handy little guidebook and
  more importantly how we can make it even handier?

Then here's your chance to tell all! Send us ideas, discoveries and
recommendations today and then look out for your valuable input
in the next edition of this title.

Email the above address (stating the title) or write to:
CitySpots Project Editor, Thomas Cook Publishing, PO Box 227,
Coningsby Road, Peterborough PE3 8SB, UK.